MILTON'S SEMITIC STUDIES

AND SOME MANIFESTATIONS OF THEM IN HIS POETRY

By

HARRIS FRANCIS FLETCHER

Assistant Professor of English
The University of Illinois

GORDIAN PRESS, INC.
NEW YORK
1966

Originally Published 1926
Reprinted by Gordian Press, Inc. 1966

Library of Congress Catalog Card No. 66-29575

Printed in U.S.A. by
EDWARDS BROTHERS, INC.
Ann Arbor, Michigan

TO MY WIFE

PREFACE

Perhaps more than any other, Milton has been generally recognized as the most learned and scholarly of all the English poets. So traditional has this conception of him become that it is today a commonplace to assume for him unlimited erudition and the possession of what for his time was a nearly universal knowledge of all fields of human action or thought. And there can be in general no quarrel with such a conception of him as a great scholarly poet; but it is high time that more accurate estimates of his learned activities should replace many of the more loosely contrived generalizations which have heretofore held sway. This is especially true in regard to Milton's Semitic studies. Masson and other biographers have, it is true, recognized the general fact of Milton's direct knowledge and use of Semitic languages, but no detailed and systematic survey of the subject has yet been made, and in most particulars the whole field of his Semitic studies is more or less a closed book.

It was in a measure to remedy this condition and to render it more nearly possible for the student of Milton to do more than generalize upon the Semitic training and equipment of the poet that this work was undertaken. I have aimed at presenting an accurate, if not wholly exhaustive, account of Milton's Semitic studies and some of the implications which arise from them, in such a way as to make it no longer necessary to speculate upon either the nature or extent of his Semitic training or study.

For guidance and assistance in much of the Semitic material employed I am indebted to Professor Leroy Waterman, of the University of Michigan.

I have also been indebted to Professor James Holly Hanford for a great deal of highly valuable advice and criticism throughout the composition of the work.

CONTENTS

CHAPTER ONE

INTRODUCTION

CHAPTER TWO

MILTON'S SEMITIC TRAINING

CHAPTER THREE

MILTON'S SEMITIC EQUIPMENT

CHAPTER FOUR

THE APPEARANCE OF SEMITIC MATERIAL IN MILTON'S POETRY

CHAPTER ONE
INTRODUCTION

I. THE PLACE OF SEMITIC STUDIES IN THE SCHOLARSHIP OF THE FIRST HALF OF THE SEVENTEENTH CENTURY

A. SEMITIC STUDIES AS A LINGUISTIC ASPECT OF THE HUMANIST TRADITION

To the heterogeneous mixture of European peoples of the early Middle Ages there slowly came the inevitably quickening force that very early began to emerge from the increasing consanguinity which a growing material prosperity produced, coupled with, and enhanced by, the larger and larger amounts of leisure and bodily ease provided by that material prosperity. New problems of morals, new problems of politics, new problems of theology arose from the operation of this force, largely through the newly acquired opportunities for noticing them as problems, and their increasing insistence made necessary some means of treating with them at once adequately and completely.

In every century of European history since the breakdown of the great Roman centralizing agency there had appeared spirits who were aware, some vaguely and some more clearly, of the operation of a centripetal urge tending to rectify and minimize the centrifugal effects of that breakdown, and each of these men contributed his bit to the formulation of that increasing awareness of new problems which eventually provided the solutions to those problems by the very intensity of that awareness. This awareness of new problems with their new implications is especially noticeable in the twelfth century, when the

3

problem of the *literae humaniores* raised itself in the work
of Hugo of St. Victor, who professed to care more for the
Christian troubles of the soul than for learning as a means
of righteousness, and who took the side of those scholastics who would read the classic authors only so far as the
actual needs of education demanded. He said:

There are two kinds of writings, first those which are termed
the *artes* proper; secondly, those which are the supplements (*appendentia*) of the *artes*. *Artes* comprise the works grouped under
(*supponuntur*) philosophy, those which contain some fixed and
determined matter of philosophy, as grammar, dialectic, and the
like. *Appendentia artium* are those [writings] which touch philosophy less nearly and are occupied with some subject apart from it;
and yet sometimes offer flotsam and jetsam from the *artes*, or
simply as narratives smooth the road to philosophy. All the songs
of poets are such—tragedies, comedies, satires, heroics, and lyrics
too, iambics, besides certain didactic works (*didascalica*), tales
likewise, and histories; also the writings of those nowadays called
philosophers, who extend a brief matter with lengthy circumlocu-
tion, and thus darken a simple meaning.

Note then well the distinction I have drawn for thee: distinct
and different (*duo*) are the *artes* and their *appenditia*, ... and
often from the latter the student will gain much labor and little
fruit. The *artes*, without their *appenditia*, may make the reader
perfect; but the latter, without the *artes*, can bring no whit of
perfection. Wherefore one should first of all devote himself to the
artes, which are so fundamental, and to the aforementioned seven
above all, which are the means and instruments (*instrumenta*) of
all philosophy. Then let the rest be read, if one has leisure, since
sometimes the playful mingled with the serious especially delights
us, and we are apt to remember a moral found in a tale.[1]

Thus, in attempting to grapple with dusty methods of
dustier scholastic educational problems, Hugo was recog-
nizing, even if slightly, the dual nature of scholastic

[1] *Didascalicon*, III, 4 (Migne, 176, cols. 768–69).

study, of which duality the sacred, rather than the secular, element had been, and was yet to be, paramount.

But as the material prosperity of Genoa, Florence, Venice, and other Mediterranean cities spread to the cities of the Hanseatic League and Paris, the human problems which the times evoked became more and more insistent. Men were more and more beginning, sporadically and gropingly, to ask questions of the scholastics which no scholastic could answer; consequently the seekers and gropers were casting about in constantly enlarging circles for some touchstone which should illumine and point out the way of release from the *impasse* which had been reached. What was needed was contact with some kindred and comprehending spirit such as only the fifteenth century provided by means of the Diaspora of Greek scholars from Constantinople in 1453. Not until then was there actually effected a veritable communion between the spirit of the present and the spirit of a past which, in its close sympathies arising from like spiritual struggles, was yet a part of the life of the present. The key to this highly energized stream of sympathetic treatment of human problems was linguistic in nature. Greek, because of the greater richness of the Greek spirit, became of the greatest importance to the intellectual life, and for the second time the Greek spirit triumphed over the Latin, swelling rapidly to such dimensions that in less than a century continental Europe became linguistically transformed. During the fifteenth century, in the reaction against scholasticism, Greek study on the Continent became the all-absorbing and all-important tool of those larger spiritual natures who wrestled with human problems. In Greek literature men found that their pressing

problems of the moment had been in some cases anticipated, in any case previously known, not as new and un-
usual problems at all, but rather as those problems which
eternally arise from the internal conflicts and strifes of a
culture or civilization which, in its lustiness of development, expands or discards old formulas and violently
creates new ones.

As the Renaissance gradually spread from Italy into
the valleys of the Seine, the Rhine, and the Rhone, it
drew more and more upon the stream of Byzantine culture. This stream, ostensibly Greek, was in reality of a
peculiar nature, for what had been originally Greek had
become fused with other streams of thought from many
sources, including Medieval mysticism, Persian astrology,
Arabian philosophy, and the Jewish mysticism which centered about the Cabbalah. These sources had become in-
extricably intermixed on the east and southeastern shores
of the Mediterranean and, when they were transferred
to the North and West, were so interwoven that Ficino
(1433–99) in his Platonic, neo-Platonic, and neo-Pytha-
gorean translations involved his fellow-scholars not only
in Greek study, but in the study of the Semitic and
Egyptian languages as well. It was as a direct result of
this peculiar nature of the source material set forth in the
Greek tongue that Pico della Mirandola and Johann
Reuchlin became deeply interested in the Semitic tongues,
and it was due to the same phenomenon that Luther later
was able to affect so markedly the contemporary stream
of theology, for his greatest work consisted in translations
of the Bible from its originals.

By the middle of the sixteenth century, or a century
later than Pico, the humanism of Italy had reached Eng-

land, and with it and because of it the study of Greek and allied, if not cognate, languages had received an immense impetus. So desultory was the study of Greek in the first quarter of the century that John Colet was hard put to it to discover for his newly refounded grammar school a master who was competent to teach the subject; but by the middle of the century there had appeared the beginnings of the greatest period of linguistic activity in English history, an activity which increased for almost exactly a century, then declined and dissipated itself into more utilitarian and linguistically secondary channels, but never completely disappeared.

In England, very early in the sixteenth century, development of linguistic study, Greek, and the Semitic tongues were caught up in the largely Protestant interest in, and attitude toward, the Scriptures, which, in its more puritanical aspect, culminated in the Authorized Version of 1611. This gigantic production, at once a result of and a further stimulus to an immensely increased attention to the Scriptures "in their original tongues" beginning in England at the dawn of the sixteenth century, paralleled the linguistic development already mentioned. The actual production of the King James Bible was rooted in the rise during the sixteenth century of the need for such a Bible, after Protestantism had become tolerated under Henry VIII, and more especially when the Puritan, with his insistence on sole and ultimate theological authority being vested in Holy Writ, was allowed at least to exist during the reign of Elizabeth. From about 1500 onward, as the Protestant attitude became more and more at home in England, such a work as the Authorized Version became inevitable; and in the production of such a work, the language or languages of the originals became of the greatest importance and interest. On these languages was now fixed the attention of the greatest scholars of the time, whether insular or continental. Erasmus, the Scaligers, Isaac Casaubon, the three great names of the Continent, became the interpreters, not only of Greek and Roman languages and literatures, but, for England, they became the great trilogy of biblical commentators whose work in some ways formed, and in others extended, the intellectual bases on which the Authorized Version was built.

The two languages, Greek and Hebrew, became the necessary tools in the erection of the great structure, and as attention became centered on them, Greek slowly came to include New Testament and Patristic Greek, while Hebrew, which at first denoted but little more than the pointed text of the Hebrew Canon, gradually took on about what is implied today in the term "Semitics." For, once set upon the task of translating the Bible "from its original tongues," English scholars lost no time in discovering and becoming familiar with those originals. The two languages gradually became the common possession of the English scholar and the man of letters, especially since at the beginning of the seventeenth century each of these designations denoted, largely, the clergy, the very group which more than any other was the most interested in, and the most concerned with, the employment of these languages.

Greek study had already taken a patristic turn on the Continent. It now proceeded to follow the same course in England. The Fathers began to be read, although there was but little done with such reading before 1600. The

interest in the study of Hebrew went forward slowly,
aided somewhat by voyagers and discoverers who jour-
neyed to the Orient and returned with plunder—merchan-
dise, manuscripts, printed books, and lore of all kinds.
The establishment, in 1547, of the Regius Professorship
in Hebrew at Cambridge was a reflection, not only of the
growing importance of Hebrew as a theological tool, but
also of an increasing interest, shared by no matter how
few, in Oriental learning and culture.

B.   SEMITIC STUDIES AS AN INSTRUMENT OF THEOLOGICAL CONTROVERSY

Despite sporadic interest, sixteenth-century study of
both Greek and Hebrew languished for a while. The time
was not yet arrived when a great impelling force should
drive scholars to the study of these two tongues, although
even thus early there was the same idolatrous attitude
adopted toward them as may be noted a half-century
later when their study reached its height. But as late as
the beginning of the seventeenth century neither language
had come in for its full share of attention, especially as
regards extensive study. For instance, in 1604 it fell to
Thomas Playfere, at that time the most distinguished
pulpit orator in the University of Cambridge, to preach
the funeral sermon of Edward Lively at St. Mary's. During the course of that sermon he insisted very emphatically upon the special claims of Hebrew on the attention of
students, as the "ancientist, the shortest, the plainest of
all languages." He went on to say:

A great part of assiduitie, as Plato sheweth, is the knowledge
of true etymologies. These in other tongues are uncertaine, in this
taking out of the naturall qualities of everything that is named.
For so much as when any man hath founde out the Hebrew

etymology, then he neede seeke no further. . . . . Therefore though a man cannot read the Rabbins, yet unless he can understande handsomely well the Hebrew text, he is compted but a maimed, or as it were but halfe a divine, especially in this learned age.[1]

Even here there is too much of the admonitory note, and in general there was as yet lacking the stimulus which the next fifty years provided for the attack, not only on Hebrew, but on Greek as well, which attack and its culmination constitute the flower of English scholarship.

The stimulus to the prodigious efforts of Protestant learning which appeared in England during the first half of the seventeenth century was the influence of Roman Catholic scholarship. The extreme Puritan view of a discipline in religion based solely on the Bible, and in most cases on the English Bible, was soon found to be ineffective against opponents like the Jesuits, who commanded every resource of biblical erudition, as well as of ecclesiastical history, for disputational purposes. As an incentive to theological controversy, this Catholic or Jesuitical scholarship reached its arrogant height in 1588–1609, in which years Cardinal Baronius, the greatest of Roman Catholic researchers, published his twelve folios of *Annales Ecclesiastici*. Mark Pattison, in his *Casaubon,* says of these *Annales:*

The whole case of the Romanists, and especially of the See of Rome, was here set out in the form of authentic annals. The *Annales* transferred to the Catholic party the preponderance in the field of learning which ever since Erasmus had been on the side of the innovators.

The task of effectively criticizing and successfully refuting Baronius' statements and arguments became the

[1] *The Felicitie of the Faithful: A Funeral Sermon Preached in St. Mary's, May 10, 1605* (Cambridge, 1621).

primary object of Protestant learning. Learning had to be met with learning, and while there is evidence which points toward this kind of controversy having appeared in England prior to this, nevertheless the situation at this time elicited a crusading zeal in which English scholars strained themselves to the utmost. However, refutation and even criticism of Baronius, in the main, had to be based on learning of a kind all too uncommon in England at that time, and Baronius was answered, not by an Englishman, but by a man who, because of the significant and devastating nature of his reply, became of intense interest and importance to Englishmen. This man was Isaac Casaubon, who perhaps more pointedly than any other single figure points precisely to the final swing of English scholarship to theological controversy with continental, rather than insular, implication.

The work of Baronius having caused this centering of linguistic studies in theological controversy, there was now provided the great impetus to the study of not only Hebrew and Greek, but of a numerous array of cognate and related languages. Greek came more and more to signify all forms of the Greek language, and specifically to include by implication New Testament, Patristic, and Byzantine Greek, not solely in order to read text or commentary, but in order that such readings might be made the bases for entrance into the vitalized discussion and dispute which assumed a knowledge of these dialects and their literatures as a prerequisite.

Hebrew, regarded by the sixteenth century as something of a literary or intellectual curiosity and studied only by the few linguistic giants of the time, who though few in number, were of a remarkable caliber, slowly began to be studied by a widening circle on a basis which was found to have been already prepared by the earlier humanists of the Renaissance. As with Greek, once the study of Hebrew was generally taken up, the term came to include cognate and related dialects and languages, with the result that the term "Hebrew" came to mean about what is meant today by the term "Semitics."

Moreover, just as Greek studies approached closer and closer to biblical literature, so, in like manner, Hebrew, which did not possess a profane literature as did Greek, became of even greater importance in theological controversy, first, because of its prime importance in reading the original text of the Old Testament; secondly, because of the new interest in, and emphasis upon, Semitic culture as a whole; and thirdly, because of the rise of that peculiar philology of the seventeenth century which wallowed through generation after generation of scholarship, acting as a "great stumbling-block" across "the threshold of the science of language"[1] until removed by Leibnitz late in the seventeenth century. I refer to the then commonly accepted philological hypothesis that Hebrew was the parent language, the root language of all languages; that all other languages were later languages which had their beginnings in the Hebrew, as it was also held that the cultures and nationalities which these languages expressed were in turn derived from Hebrew culture. This, before Leibnitz, was the be-all and end-all of the science or study of philology, and is of importance here because of the indication it affords of the hold Semitic study had secured on the scholarship of the time.

[1] Max Müller, *The Science of Language.*

II. THE NATURE OF MILTON'S CONTACTS
WITH SEMITIC STUDY

During the first quarter of the seventeenth century the program for all education in England, except the most rudimentary, pointed largely in the direction of the church. Most youths for whom even a grammar school education was projected were tacitly assumed to be beginning a process which would eventually end in taking orders. So almost wholly was the higher education of the time directed toward the church that in 1602 the "learned" John Selden left Oxford, never to return, to enter an inn of chancery. The virulent nature of his inflammatory *History of Tithes* which appeared in 1618 was an indication that university education of the time afforded little opportunity for legal training or training other than theological.

The education of the time was arranged primarily for prospective priests of the Church of England; and, as has already been indicated, theological training had gradually come to assume, if it did not require, thorough linguistic preparation with increasing emphasis upon the biblical tongues. All that was necessary for a youth of the early seventeenth century to be brought in contact with Semitic study was to send the boy to a grammar school and then to Oxford or Cambridge, where, if the youth really desired to take advantage of his opportunities, he could become as proficient as his own ability and the scholarship of the time would permit.

It was almost inevitable that Milton should have

avidly seized upon all forms of linguistic study with which
he came in contact, for there were in his case two powerful
factors operating in that direction from the very beginning of his education. The first of them was his father's
avowed purpose and endeavor to place at his son's dis-
posal the best educational advantages which the time
afforded, and secondly, Milton's peculiarly scholarly
nature. To the first of these must be ascribed the opportunity which was afforded him for contact with the full
humanistic stream of intellectual learning and interests,
beginning with St. Paul's school and continuing on
through the sojourn in Italy until his establishment in the
house in Aldergate Street. Every advantage for linguistic
study was set before him; every encouragement was forthcoming from his solicitous father for the completion in the
fullest measure of the best training which England could
offer her more fortunate sons, and, when that was com-
pleted, the "grand tour" came as a culmination that was
also the finishing touch to a linguistic education already
replete with the best that England could offer.

This magnificent opportunity for education was seized
upon by a nature which naturally yearned for, and em-
braced, learning of every description, and which had done
so since its earliest years. Milton's early friendship with
his tutor, Thomas Young; the "lady" epithet; the elegy
and epistles to Charles Diodati—all speak of a nature
which held itself consciously aloof, not so much because
of youthful priggishness, although that element was present in him, but rather because of a sort of a premonitional
consciousness of purpose coupled with that eager curiosity
to learn which is but lightly concealed in his earlier work.
The very early high consciousness of the priestlike char-

acter of his conception of the rôle of the creative artist, set forth in the Diodati elegy, affords ample opportunity for gaining an insight into the nature of the driving force within the man which enabled him to secure the fullest returns from the educational opportunities presented to him.

The Semitic nature of his educational development is in its general features known to everyone, but its implications remain *terra incognita*. The conventionally observed facts are as follows:

Milton's study of the Semitic dialects must have begun at a rather early date, for at least as early as March of 1625 he was thanking Thomas Young for the gift of a Hebrew Bible, "long since gratefully received," in the first "Familiar Epistle" of March 26, 1625. As he received this Bible after he had matriculated but before he had taken residence at Cambridge it is likely that his Semitic studies were well along by that time.

The influence of Cambridge was toward an extensive, rather than an intensive, expansion of his linguistic equipment, as is evidenced in a letter to Alexander Gill, when, to the statement that he is inclosing an ode in Greek heroic verse, he adds, "I must inform you that from the time I left your school [St. Paul's] this is the first and the last piece I have ever composed in Greek." His actual contacts with Semitics at Cambridge may only be conjectured; but the college Latin exercise *De Idea Platonica Quemadmodum Aristoteles Intellexit*, containing the reference to Hermes Trismegistus, is further evidence of his Cambrian contact with Oriental lore and reading.

During the Horton period Milton confesses to an immense amount of reading:

On my father's estate, where he had determined to pass the remainder of his days, I enjoyed an interval of uninterrupted leisure, which I entirely devoted to the perusal of the Greek and Latin classics; though I occasionally visited the metropolis either for the sake of purchasing books or of learning something new in mathematics or in music, in which I, at that time, found a source of pleasure and amusement. In this manner I spent five years till my mother's death.[1]

He does not mention Semitic reading during this period, but his activities upon his return from Italy indicate that he must have employed some of his abundant leisure at Horton in Semitic study, for in the early forties he introduced his nephews to Semitic study, as Phillips states that he was taught "the Hebrew, Chaldee, and Syriack, so far as to go through the Pentateuch, or five books of Moses in Hebrew, to make a good entrance into the Targum or Chaldee Paraphrase, and to understand several chapters of St. Mathew in the Syriack Testament."[2]

His pamphleteering, begun about the same time, contains evidence that he was doing a large amount of Semitic study, including the reading of some documents in various Semitic languages, the reading of others in Latin translation, and the reading of works on various phases of Semitic civilization, written by Europeans. The tractate *Of Education*, of 1644, with its elaboration of a scheme of education, confirms Phillips' statement concerning the Semitic languages taught by Milton the tutor.

A few years later, in 1648, appeared a most tangible bit of evidence of his Semitic labors in the form of the *Nine Psalms Done into Metre*, which he professed to be as

[1] *Defensio Secunda.*

[2] Phillips' *Life.*

literal a translation from the Hebrew original as the metrical arrangement would permit.

The innumerable biblical references which appear throughout the prose and directly refer to the Hebrew text reach their maximum in the *De Doctrina Christiana*, the last great prose work; but his reading of the Hebrew scriptures continued daily until his death.

III. THE PROBLEMS ARISING FROM MILTON'S CONTACTS WITH SEMITIC STUDIES

The work which I propose to do will be first to point out the general linguistic training of the youth of Milton's time, with special reference to the field of Semitics, and secondly, to present Milton's connection with such training. Then, having summarily surveyed the field of English education during the first quarter of the seventeenth century and having presented the known facts of Milton's connection with that educational stream, with special consideration for his training in Semitics, there will arise a number of problems which will require definite solutions; among others, these three:

1. The problem of Milton's proficiency in the Semitic languages, the treatment of which should determine with some degree of completeness those oriental languages with which he was familiar. I propose in this connection to attempt to determine not only what languages he knew, but also to indicate those which he knew well and those which were known but casually. It is high time that something more be said of Milton's Semitics than, as Johnson put it, "he knew Hebrew, with its two dialects"; for I doubt if Johnson knew exactly what he meant by the "two dialects." At any rate, no one since has known with any degree of certainty.

2. Furthermore, there is the possibility of pointing out much more clearly just what his acquaintance was with Semitic literatures and documents, on the one hand, and his acquaintance with contemporary, or, more strictly,

European commentary or research work upon Semitic literature, on the other hand. In other words, I intend to indicate as specifically as possible the range of his knowledge of Semitic literatures and of criticism, in its broadest sense, of those literatures.

3. Then, having cleared the ground in this manner, there remains the task of pointing out some of the Semitic elements found in his poetry. In order to do this, some preliminary consideration is necessary of what is meant by "Semitic influence" or "Semitic material," as these terms are here being used. By such phrases I do not mean such influence or material as would have functioned in the work of the conventional biblical scholar of Milton's own or any other day. Not such influence or material as an Englishman of Milton's time might have obtained from study of the Bible with a knowledge of Latin and Greek; not even such influence or material as would have come to him from a knowledge of classical Hebrew, important and influential though that would have been; and not such biblical contacts as would have come through the training accorded any English divine of that time in Anglican theology—none of these nor all of them would have, nor could have, supplied a clearly marked influence or body of material which would have been genuinely Semitic in nature, untinctured by previous contacts with European treatments.

Rather, I shall mean by "Semitic influence" or "material" such influence or material which could only have been acquired by a scholar interested as Milton was in manuscripts,[1] who would have used full scholiastic

---

[1] "You afterwards obligingly admitted me into the Museum, you permitted me to see the repository of literature and many Greek manu-

equipment for his study of the LXX and the Vulgate, and who would have insisted on augmenting such study with similar work on the Hebrew canon itself, using the fullest scholiastic equipment to which he had access, including Aramaic and rabbinical versions of scripture along with their scholiastical commentary. Furthermore, in addition to the use of Semitic scholiasts, there should appear, in order to secure genuine Semitic material or influence, some evidence of Milton's having known and used much of the Semitic material which remained largely un-christianized, such as the massoretic, rabbinical, and other more or less obscure writings of Jewish scholars of the Middle Ages and Renaissance.

----

scripts. . . . ." ("Familiar Epistle" of March 30, 1639, to Luke Holstein in the Vatican.) Cf. also *De Doctrina*, cap. V, *De Filio Dei*, comment on I John 5:7.

CHAPTER TWO
MILTON'S SEMITIC TRAINING

I. THE BEGINNINGS

Milton's general linguistic training began very early in his life, as the following references indicate.

At *thy* cost, worthiest father,
When I had mastered fully the tongue of the Romans, and tasted
Latin delights enough, and the speech for which Jove's mouth
    was moulded,
That grand speech of the Greeks which served for their great
    elocution
Thou 'twas advised the vaunted flowers of Gaul in addition,
Thereto the language in which the new and fallen Italian
Opens his lips with sounds that attest the Barbarian inroads,
Yea, and the mystic strains which the Palestine prophet delivers.[1]

I must say therefore, that after I had for my first years, by the ceaseless diligence of my father, been exercised to the tongues . . . . as my age would suffer. . . . .[2]

My father destined me from a child to the pursuits of literature . . . . [my father] then, after I had acquired a proficiency in various languages, ... sent me to the University of Cambridge.[3]

All of these references to his language training emphasize the early age at which he began to be "exercised in the tongues," and this emphasis greatly simplifies the problem of determining his acquaintanceship with any particular language, for any problem which concerns his early language training now becomes quite definitely related to the linguistic training of the youth of the first

---

[1] *Ad Patrem* (Masson's translation), written at about the beginning of the Horton period, or in the early 1630's, David Masson, *Life of Milton*, I (1859–94), 336.

[2] *The Reason of Church Government Urged against Prelaty* (1641).

[3] *Defensio Secunda* (1654).

quarter of the seventeenth century, and whatever is known about the general linguistic procedure of the time becomes of significance here.

The training in the languages appears to have been well started before 1625, or before Milton took residence at Cambridge: "[My father], then, after I had acquired a proficiency in various languages, sent me to the University of Cambridge."[1]

To that period of his life before his departure from London for Cambridge must, therefore, be assigned the groundwork of Milton's language study. The languages studied may very properly be inferred from the list supplied by the *Ad Patrem* passage already quoted, viz., Latin, Greek, French, Italian, and Hebrew.[2]

From all of these references to his language training it becomes quite clearly evident, first, that his training began very early, and secondly, that certain definite languages were studied and, to quite a large extent in each case, definitely mastered by the time he entered Cambridge. There remains the necessity for determining the process by means of which all of this language study was accomplished.

It is well to remember at this point that his education before Cambridge was quite definitely dominated by three major influences which, in the order of their chronological functionings, were: first, his father; secondly, Thomas Young, his tutor; and thirdly, St. Paul's School. The first two of these influences are obviously individuals,

[1] *Op. cit.*

[2] Professor Hanford has suggested that the order of listing of these languages represents the order of acquisition. Certainly Milton often enough supplies ample instances of such dual purpose listings.

and the third also became individualized for Milton through Alexander Gill the younger, as the later correspondence between the two would indicate.[1] A great deal of attention must therefore be devoted to these three figures, because of the effect they severally produced upon Milton's linguistic development.

His father was responsible for the guidance into the "pursuits of literature" and the "various tongues," as Milton himself says in the *Defensio Secunda:* "My father destined me from a child to the pursuits of literature, ... had me daily instructed . . . . in various languages." The *Ad Patrem* is one long eulogy of his father as the one person above all others to whom he owed not only his education, but even his inspiration. The encouragement which Milton must have received from his father to begin the study of "the tongues" was of vast importance for both the direction and the nature of that language study. Not many commoners of the early seventeenth century would have permitted their sons the luxury of almost unlimited language study; fewer still would have deliberately suggested such study.

Though Milton's father is thus so signally and specifically singled out and acclaimed for his part in Milton's early education, other important influences are not entirely neglected. Milton says: ". . . . After I had for my first years . . . . been exercised to the tongues, and some sciences, as my age would suffer, by sundry masters and teachers both at home and at the schools" (*Reason of Church Government*). And again: "My father had me daily instructed in the grammar school, and by other masters at home" (*Defensio Secunda*). From these two

[1] Cf. *Familiar Epistles* II, III, and IV.

statements it may be concluded that the study at grammar school was concomitant with study with "other masters at home," and that the two processes went forward together. Probably such was actually the case after his twelfth year, for if his statement in the famous *Of Education* tractate be borne in mind to the effect that a "complete and generous education" may be secured "between twelve and twenty," there is produced a lower age limit, of a kind, for his age when entering grammar school. However, as boys were not admitted to St. Paul's until they could read and write,[1] Milton had, by the time he entered St. Paul's, become well acquainted with private tutors.

[1] In a letter written apparently after the death of Colet, from Erasmus to Justus Ionas, Erasmus says, "He [Colet] divided the school into four apartments. The first, viz., the Porch and Entrance, is for Catechumens, for the children to be instructed in the principles of Religion; *where no child is to be admitted but what can read and write.*" The meaning of this points clearly to the fact that from its foundation by Colet, St. Paul's admitted only boys who had instruction at home or by private tutors.

II. THOMAS YOUNG

Except from Aubrey,[1] there is but one of the "sundry masters at home" of whom there is a distinct account as having been one of Milton's masters before he went to grammar school and by whom he was taught privately while attending such a school. This was Thomas Young, Puritan minister in Suffolk, and well known in later life as a prominent member of the Puritan party.

Young was a Scotchman by birth, as in one of his later publications he signs himself *Theophilus Philo-Kuriaces, Loncardiensis*, which, freely translated gives, "Theophilus Kirklover, Loncardy." Masson, with his indefatigable sifting, discovers this place to be Loncardy in Perthshire, more frequently spelled "Loncarty."[2] From Young's epitaph, which states that he died in 1655, aged sixty-eight, he appears to have been born at Loncardy in 1587 or 1588. He was sent from there to the University of St. Andrew's, where his name is found among the matriculations of St. Leonard's College in 1602.[3] As he was incorporated into the M.A. degree at Cambridge in 1644 *apud Sancti Andrianos*, he must have finished his arts education at the Scotch university, and probably became a licentiate of the Scottish kirk. Just how he occupied himself or where he was located during the period between his severing connections with St. Andrew's and his appearing as tutor to the young Milton

[1] Aubrey, *Brief Lives*, ed. Clark, II (Oxford, 1898), 63.

[2] Masson, *op. cit.*, I, 68.

[3] *Op. cit.*, I, 70 and note, p. 71.

is not known, although Masson, as usual, throws out a number of interesting conjectures, and concludes them with this statement: "By the chances of the time, and the search after a livelihood, it had fallen to a wandering Scot from Loncardy, bred to hardy literature amid the sea-breezes of St. Andrew's, to be the domestic preceptor of the future English poet." Masson further surmises, from the probability that Young was already married, that he did not reside with his pupil, but only visited him daily.

There is some uncertainty as to when Young first assumed his preceptorial duties; but if, as Aubrey related, Milton was writing verses when but ten year old, undoubtedly his father would have felt the need of a tutor for him even before that age, which would have been two or three years before the time, 1620, when he is usually assumed to have started to grammar school. The relationship with Young would have then begun about 1617, and would have continued until Young left England in 1622 to become chaplain to the English merchants at Hamburg.

From the tutor-pupil relationship of the two grew a dual bond of attachment. One aspect of this bond was the love and friendship which sprang up between this matured, university-trained cleric and the eager, exquisitely adjusted adolescent, and which has been preserved in the two letters and the Latin elegy written to Young. The other outstanding aspect of the bond between them, preserved also in the writings to Young, was the linguistic interests which they held in common, induced and guided by the tutor.

Perhaps the personal relations which existed between them should be considered first, as this relationship constituted Milton's first experience with a tutor, and it apparently set a precedent for subsequent tutor relationships. The two letters (*Familiar Epistles* I and IV) are all that are left of what was evidently a lengthy, if not a voluminous, correspondence. In the first of these letters, written from London, March 26, 1625, Milton speaks of the "incredible and singular gratitude" he owed Young, and calls heaven to witness that he has not written him for three years, and that the reason for not writing has been that he did not wish to "tease" him with his compositions. Milton then adds, almost in a spirit of bantering levity: "And I was anxious that if my letters had nothing else to commend them, they might be commended by their rarity." The tone of the remainder of the letter would indicate clearly that the friendliest and most intimate relations existed between the two.

The second surviving letter, written from Cambridge, July 21, 1628, is of the same general familiar tone as the first. Milton again is full of apology for his neglect of the correspondence between them, and refuses to permit Young to blame himself for this negligence: "How can I, or ought I, to expect that you should always have leisure enough from more serious engagements to write to me, particularly when it is kindness, and not duty, which prompts you to write?" In this same letter Milton thanks Young for an invitation to visit him, and accepts the invitation.[1]

[1] Cf. Rev. A. G. H. Hollingsworth, *The History of Stowmarket* (London, 1844), p. 193. Hollingsworth conjectures that not only did Milton make this visit to Stowmarket, but that the relationship was never allowed to lapse, being revived for the last time during Milton's residence in Petty France, Westminster, in 1653, after he had become totally blind.

The Latin elegy to Young only serves to add to the sense of intimate relationship which the two letters so clearly show. Milton addresses Young as:

The other half of my soul, yea, more; without him I am forced to live half a life. Ah me, how many seas, how many mountains, interpose to part me from my other self! Dearer to me he is than wert thou, Socrates, wisest of Greeks, to Alcibiades, who had Telamon for ancestor; dearer than the great Stagyrite to his generous pupil, Alexander, whom Olympias of Chaonia bore to Lybian Jove. As to the king of the Myrmidons was the son of Amyntor, or Cheiron, son of nymph Philyra, such is this man to me.

The first aspect of the relationship which existed between Milton and Young is, then, the peculiarly intimate friendship which grew up between them.

The second aspect of their relationship which is significant is the emphasis which this friendship put upon all manners of linguistic interests. Milton employs Latin as the communicating medium when writing Young, although both men were Englishmen. The *Elegia* is loaded with literary allusion taken from the literature which Young had introduced to him. Milton expressly states his indebtedness to Young in this respect, when he says: "I followed his footsteps when I first wandered through the hollows of the Aonian mount, and through the sacred groves of the cloven hill; with him I first drank the waters of the Pierian spring, and under favor of Clio wet my happy lips thrice with wine of Castaly."[1] Such a linguistic bond between them would almost inevitably have led to considerations of language study very early in their acquaintance, discussions of what languages to pursue,

[1] Milton's fourth Latin elegy is usually dated 1627. It should be dated 1624–25. Cf. my correspondence in the *Times Literary Supplement*, No. 1253 (January 21, 1926), 44.

what to emphasize, together with some sampling of the various languages discussed. In such a way as this Hebrew study was probably discussed and tasted. Certain it is that Young, because of his theological training at St. Andrew's, knew Hebrew, as it was required of all students of divinity in Scotch universities after 1560;[1] and as the other languages listed in the *Ad Patrem* list were begun with Young as tutor, the probability is that Hebrew was among them in reality, as it is by inference on the basis of that *Ad Patrem* list.

[1] Cf. John Knox, "First Book of Discipline," *The Works of John Knox*, edited by David Laing, II (Edinburgh, 1864), 213.

III. ST. PAUL'S SCHOOL

Like most boys of his time who were of sufficiently well-to-do families to permit more than the barest educational accomplishments, Milton's first experience with an organized educational institution was in grammar school.

The most important grammar schools of London at the time Milton was old enough to enter were St. Paul's, in St. Paul's Churchyard, a successor to the old Cathedral school of St. Paul's which had existed in the same place from time immemorial;[1] Westminster School, founded anew by Elizabeth in continuation of the older monastic school which had existed in Catholic times, and where Ben Jonson, George Herbert, and Giles Fletcher, all then alive, had been educated, and where Camden, after serving as under-master, had held the office of headmaster since 1592; St. Anthony's Free School, in Threadneedle Street, where Sir Thomas More and Archbishop Whitgift had been educated; and the free school of the Merchant Tailors' Company, founded in 1561.

Milton entered the oldest and most famous of these, that of St. Paul's, it being but a short distance from his home in Bread Street. The origin of this school is usually confused with its re-endowment, in or about 1510, by

[1] Of St. Paul's School before Colet there is quite a literature, centering around Leach's researches in the early years of the twentieth century. Cf. *Journal of Education* (London, June-July, 1908; June, 1904; July, 1909); Walter Besant, *London, the City* (1910), pp. 385 ff.; and A. F. Leach, the *Times* (April 12, 21, 1904; July 7, 14, August 3, 1909); *Archaeologia*, LXII, 191; *Classical Review*, XXIV, 146; also his *Schools of Medieval England* (London, 1910), pp. 109 ff. and 277 ff.

John Colet (1467?–1519), then dean of St. Paul's. Of the famous statutes which have been accorded such an exalted place in the development of English public school education, it will be enough to note here that in them Colet refrained from precise statement of curricula: "What shal be taught it passith my wit to devyse and determine in particular." But "in general" he would that the pupils were taught "all way in good literature with Laten and greke and goode auctors such as have the veray romayne eliquence joyned withe wisdome, especially Cristyn auctors that wrote theyre wysdome with clene and chast laten in other verse or in prose."[1] For he said that his great aim was to increase knowledge and "good Cristen lyff and maners," conduct and character being with him, as with his predecessors, the first object. He therefore put first the English *Catechism*, which he himself had written, then Erasmus' *Institute of a Christian*, and then "other auctores Christen," adding such other authors as should most conduct to true Latin speaking.

From Lily, first headmaster under Colet's foundation, whose Latin grammar was still in use long after Milton's time, stretches a period of great importance in the history of St. Paul's school, through the headmasterships of John Rightwis, Lily's successor and son-in-law, Jones, Freeman, Cook, Malin, Harrison, and Richard Mulcaster, to the appointment in 1608 of Alexander Gill the elder.[2] During this time there were many changes made in the school, especially in additions made to the curriculum.

[1] Nicholas Carlisle, *A Concise Description of the English Grammar Schools* II (London, 1818), 70 ff.

[2] *Op. cit.*, pp. 94–95.

Among the innovations in English grammar-school education which took place between the time of Colet's foundation of St. Paul's and Milton's entry therein was the introduction of Hebrew into the grammar-school curriculum. Hebrew had made its first appearance, in a school curriculum of which there is a record, at York School, in January of 1546–47, when, late in the reign of Henry the Eighth, this school was established by deed, in which deed was specified that the master was to be "convenientlie seen and have understandinge in the Hebrew, Greek, and Latin tongues."[1] From this time on there were sporadic appearances of the language as a school subject for study in grammar school curricula, among which may be noted the following records of such appearances:

East Retford grammar school (1552): Form IV boys were to learn Hebrew grammar.

Westminster School: In the early days, *ca.* 1560 onward, Hebrew grammar in seventh form with a lesson from the Psalter in both Greek and Hebrew. Busby's own Grammar, "multiplied in MSS?" and not published until 1708, was the textbook.

Newport grammar school (Essex, 1589): Dr. Legge's orders for the government of the school required Hebrew to be taught, together with Latin and Greek.

Heath grammar school (*ca.* 1600): By statute, the Master of the School was required to teach the boys Hebrew.

It may be noted that (*ca.* 1635): Hebrew was in-

---

[1] A. F. Leach, *op. cit.*, p. 328.

tended to be part of the curriculum in the projected *Museum Minervae* of Sir Francis Kynaston.[1]

Specific evidence for the progress of Hebrew as a school subject at St. Paul's is lacking, having been, with the rest of the school's records, destroyed by fire. But the study of the subject appears to have reached its height during the headmastership of Richard Mulcaster, the immediate predecessor of Gill, who was noted for his Semitic scholarship, being spoken of by Hugh Broughton as "one of the best Hebrew scholars of the age."

Milton himself supplies important evidence for his grammar-school study of Hebrew in his tractate *Of Education*, in the familiar passage: "And ere this time the Hebrew tongue at a set hour might have been gained, that the Scriptures may be now read in their own original: whereto it would be no impossibility to add the Chaldee, and the Syriac dialect." As Milton specifies the beginning age to be twelve years, the "ere this time" implies a rather early commencement of Semitic study. There is much more reason for this course of study to be autobiographical than has been supposed, for comment on the passage has chiefly pointed out the extravagance of the implied requirement. Commentators have exclaimed[2] at the "Miltonic rigor" of the entire course of study, and at the mention of Semitics have felt that the entire scheme has been made improbable if not impossible. But for Milton's time such a program was neither overelaborate

[1] Foster Watson, *The English Grammar Schools to 1660* (Cambridge, 1908), pp. 529 ff.

[2] Samuel Johnson was especially skeptical of the efficacy of Milton's vaunted method, and criticized it at some length, both as to content and as to procedure.

nor pretentious, given a thorough tutor and apt pupils, and certainly these conditions were met in the Young-Milton relationship if the classical and literary allusion in the writings to Young be any sufficient criterion. In all probability Milton was only rearranging his own procedure in his youth, to a certain extent, for there is a good parallel to his projected curriculum preserved, written at an earlier date than the *Of Education* tractate.

This work was entitled *A New Discovery of the Old Art of Teaching*,[1] and was written by Charles Hoole. Hoole was born in Yorkshire in 1610. He was educated at Wakefield free school and at Lincoln College, Oxford, where he proceeded Bachelor of Arts in 1634 and Master of Arts in 1636.[2] He took holy orders about 1632, and was appointed master of the free school of Rotherham in Yorkshire. He became rector of Great Ponton, Lincolnshire, in 1642, and was sequestered by the Parliament. He thereupon came to London, where he made himself a name as a tutor. He taught at private schools in a house near Maidenhead Court in Aldergate Street,[3] where, in Wood's phrase, "the generalitie of the youth were instructed to a miracle." He lived through the Interregnum

[1] Charles Hoole, *A New Discovery of the Old Art of Teaching*, "shewing how children in their playing years may grammatically attain to a firm groundedness in, and exercise of, the Latine, Greek, and Hebrew Tongues. Written about twenty-three years ago for the benefit of Rotherham School, where it was first used" (London, 1660, reprint of Syracuse, New York, 1912), written about 1637 or 1636.

[2] Wood, *Fasti*, I, 465 ff.

[3] Hoole taught in a house between Goldsmith's Alley, in Red Cross Street, and Maidenhead Court, in Aldergate Street, from 1642 until 1651 (cf. Hoole, D. N. B. art. and *Notes and Queries*, 6th series, VI, 89 and 134). It may be noted that this residence threw him into close proximity with Milton during the latter's residence in Aldergate Street, 1640–45.

and was made rector of Stock, Essex, in 1660, where he died in 1666–67. The *New Discovery* was but one of many educational works written during his lifetime, some of which were published after his death.

This *New Discovery* is a work which greatly increases our knowledge of grammar school methods of the first half of the seventeenth century. Hoole states that "it is usual in Cities and greater Towns to put children to Schoole about four or five years of age, and in Country villages, because of further distance, not till about six or seven."[1] He begins the process of education with the study of English, and at "seven or eight years of age, a child may begin Latine."[2] Greek began in the fourth form, and became the basis for Hebrew, which he taught in the sixth form regularly, although sometimes begun in the fifth. His introductory remarks on the approach to the study of Hebrew[3] make Milton's scheme appear much

[1] Hoole, *op. cit.*, p. 29.

[2] *Ibid.*, p. 53.

[3] *Ibid.*, p. 197: "Though it may seem a needlesse labour to prescribe directions for the teaching of the two upper forms, partly because I find more written concerning them (lost to us) than the rest, and partly because many very eminent and able Schoole-Masters employ most of their pains in perfecting them, every one making use of such Authors, and such a Method as in his own discretion he judgeth meetest to make them Scholars; not to say, that the Scholars themselves (being not well acquainted with the Latine and Greek Grammar, and having gotten a good understanding (at least) of the Latine Tongue, by the frequent exercise of translating, and speaking Latine, and writing Colloquies, Epistles, Historical and Fabulous narrations and the like, besides reading some Schoole Authors, and other helpful and profitable books, will be able in many things to proceed without a guide, addicting their mindes chiefly to those studies, which their natural Genius doth most prompt them to, either concerning Oratory or Poetry; yet I think it requisite for me to go on as I have begun, and to shew what course I have constantly kept

less ambitious, especially when the different ages of the two sets of pupils are considered, Milton's imagined pupils being much older than Hoole's actual ones.

Hoole then sets forth the method which he, as a practical schoolmaster, has employed in the teaching of Hebrew.[1] As a method, it represents what Hoole was actually doing in his teaching a scant ten years after Milton had left St. Paul's.[2] Hoole gives ample evidence that neither the method nor the subject was of the nature of a complete innovation which had crept in during those ten years by his references to other pedagogical procedure, especially that of Richard Mulcaster, already mentioned as the predecessor of Gill as headmaster at St. Paul's.[3] Hoole proposed to introduce his pupils to the study of Hebrew at the beginning of the fifth form, which would have been at the age of thirteen or fourteen, in order that the study might proceed as a preparation for use later at the university. He has outlined his exact method of beginning the subject, mentioned and discussed various textbooks in current use, and indicated what further work might be attempted if the amount ordinarily allotted proved insufficient.

His ordinary allotment for the fifth and sixth forms

---

with these two forms, to make them exactly compleat in the Greek and Latine Tongues, and as perfect Orators, and Poets in both as their young years and capacities will suffer; and to enter them so in Hebrew, as that they may be able to proceed themselves in that holy Language, whether they go to the University or are otherwise disposed on to some necessary calling, which their Parents or Friends think fitting for them."

[1] Hoole, *op. cit.*, pp. 214 ff.

[2] Watson, *op. cit.*, p. 529.

[3] *Ibid.*, p. 528.

was the introduction to grammar, using Buxtorf's *Epitome*[1] as a text, which he held to be better for beginner's purposes than those of Bellarminus, Martinius, or Amama.[2] The grammar work comprised the writing of the letters and the "chief rules," the learning of what little declensional vestiges are remaining in Hebrew, together with the pronomial paradigms, the paradigms of the conjugations with their "proper meanings," and the daily memorizing of a certain number of roots.

The pupils were then to examine texts from the Pentateuch, which they were required to parse, construe, and be able to write in Hebrew from the English or Latin. After sufficient practise in this work, they began their first translation, which was the Psalms. For this work he recommends the lexicon of Buxtorf or Pagnine.[3] When the Psalms had been finished, he proceeded to the Proverbs, Ecclesiastes, and Job, in the order named. At this point he proposed to introduce a large amount of "exercise" work, which meant the writing of "orations," verses, and epistles in Hebrew. Hoole here mentions the fact that at that time the students of Westminster School were able to produce orations and verse, not only in Hebrew, but "in Arabick and other Oriental Tongues, to the amazement of their hearers, who are angry at their own ignorance, because they know not well what is then being said or written." As equipment for such exercises

[1] Johann Buxtorf I, *Praecysta (Epitome) Gramm. Hebr.* (Basel, 1605, 1613).

[2] Robertus Bellarminus, *Institutiones Linguae Hebraicae* (Rome, 1578, 1580); Petrus Martinius, *Gramm. Hebr. Libri* II (Paris, 1568); Sixtus Amama, *Gramm. Hebr. Martinio-Buxtorfiana* (Amsterdam, 1625).

[3] Johann Buxtorf I. *Lexicon Hebr.-Chald.* (Basel, 1607); Sanctus Pagninus, *Epitome Thesauri Linguae Sacrae* (Antwerp, 1570).

he mentions the lexicons of Schindler, Buxtorf, Pagnine, Trost, and the *Aviani Clavis Poeseos Sacrae.*[1]

He ordinarily concluded the work in Hebrew at this point, but if occasion arose for going further, he proposed that the student now proceed, by the aid of the equipment thus far acquired, to the study of those other "Tongues in which portions of the Bible are written, Hebrew, Chaldee, Samaritane, Syriack, Arabick, Persian, Aethiopick, Armenian, and Coptick, which is a kind of Aegyptian Tongue."

This, as a method, represented what Hoole, as a practical schoolmaster, was doing with Hebrew as a school subject a scant ten years after Milton left St. Paul's. He gives ample evidence by his references to like pedagogical procedure, especially that of Richard Mulcaster,[2] that neither the method nor the subject were completely revolutionary in English grammar-school curricula. That Hoole was an exceptionally good tutor is evident from any consideration whatever of his book, and furthermore the probability is that he was fortunate in his acquisition of scholars; and such an ambitious program as he outlines would require above all else a tutor of rare qualities and pupils of rare capacities.

Milton's scheme for introducing Semitic study early in school life, in the light of Hoole, points now much more emphatically to an autobiographical origin than heretofore, for the possibility of at least the beginning of Hebrew

---

[1] Valentine Schindler, *Lexicon Pentaglotton Hebr.*, *Chald.*, *Syr.*, *Talmudico-Rabbin.*, *et Arab.* (Frankfort, 1612); Martinus Trostius, *Gramm. Heb. Universalis* (Copenhagen, 1627); Hieronymus Avianus, *Clovis Poeseos Sacrae* (Leipzig, 1627).

[2] Mulcaster has already been referred to as the predecessor of the elder Gill as headmaster at St. Paul's.

study at St. Paul's or during the St. Paul's period is much more clearly indicated. Not only does the probability of the subject having been taught there become much more of a certainty from a consideration of Hoole's work, but the further requirement of an extraordinary tutor, for such teaching to be of any great value, has been met, as has been shown, in Milton's early tutor, Thomas Young.[1]

The insistence of the autobiographical references to the language training "in early youth," the connection with a first-rate tutor who was also linguistically inclined, and the indication that Hebrew was a grammar school subject by the most nearly contemporary direct exposition which has been preserved of the exact grammar-school treatment of Hebrew as a school subject—all of these elements point with increasing insistence to Milton having acquired, before Cambridge, some considerable amount of groundwork in the Hebrew tongue.

[1] Phillips, in his *Life of Milton*, yields some curious evidence of the actual application of the outline in the tractate to the education of himself and his brother, John, as conducted by Milton. After elaborating the work done in Greek and Latin, he says: "Nor did the time thus studiously employed in conquering the Greek and Latin tongues hinder the attaining to the chief Oriental languages, viz., the Hebrew, Chaldee, and Syriack, so far as to go through the Pentateuch, or five books of Moses in Hebrew, to make a good entrance into the Targum or Chaldee Paraphrase, and to understand several chapters of St. Mathew in the Syriack Testament." This is a skeletal outline of the work of Hoole.

IV. CAMBRIDGE

A. AN ACCOUNT OF SEMITIC STUDY
AT CAMBRIDGE

Milton's first contact with the stream of linguistic study and theological interests was made through his two early tutors, Thomas Young and Alexander Gill the Younger. He did not, however, come in full and complete contact with that stream, which was briefly outlined in chapter i, until he reached Cambridge. Upon his taking residence at the University there began that remarkable alignment with European scholarship in general and linguistic scholarship in particular, which process the Italian journey so greatly aided.

By 1625, the year of Milton's matriculation at Cambridge, there was greater opportunity for Semitic study than ever before in the history of the University. Hebrew, up to, and even after, the appearance of the Authorized Version, had been rather neglected and slighted at Cambridge.[1] However, there had been an increasingly larger attention accorded to the study of Semitics beginning with the establishment of the Regius Professorship of Hebrew in 1547, and the later years of the sixteenth century saw the chairs of both Hebrew and Greek filled by eminent scholars whose extreme length of office was perhaps justified by their fitness for the duties of that office. Of the two languages, Hebrew undoubtedly received the greater share of attention, and, from its first appearance as a recognized subject, did not lack com-

[1] Cf. Mullinger, *History of Cambridge*, II, 417.

petent expositors. The first professor of Hebrew was Thomas Wakefield, who, for some reason or other, did not lecture during his term of office, although his ability and learning were unquestioned. But during the reign of Edward, and again in that of Elizabeth, readers were appointed to lecture in his stead. Among these were names to conjure with in European scholarship of the time. The first lecturer was the unfortunate Paulus Fagius, who accompanied Martin Bucer to Cambridge in 1549. Born in the Palatinate in 1504, he received his early education from his father, who was a schoolmaster. At the age of eleven he was sent to Heidelberg, and at eighteen, removed to Strasburg, where he was obliged to resort to tuition to defray expenses. He devoted whatever leisure he could spare to the acquisition of the Hebrew language. His teacher was the famous Wolfgang Capito, by whose assistance he rapidly gained great proficiency in that tongue. In 1527 he settled in Isne as a schoolmaster, where he married and had a family. About 1537 he took holy orders and gained a considerable reputation as a preacher of the reformed doctrines. During all this time he had kept up his Semitic studies, and availed himself of the ablest assistance, in particular, that of the celebrated rabbi, Elias Levita, whom he induced to come to Isne from Venice. Peter Buffler, one of the senators of Isne, enabled Fagius to erect a printing press at Isne for the printing of Hebrew books. From this press oriental literature received many valuable additions. He was summoned to Heidelberg in 1546 to promote the Protestant religion, but Protestants in Germany being hotly persecuted, Fagius, accompanied by Martin Bucer, came to England in April, 1549, in compliance with an invitation from Archbishop Cranmer, with the sanction of the Lord-Protector Somerset. After having been entertained for a short time at Lambeth palace, the two were appointed by the privy council to reside in Cambridge University for the purpose of teaching Semitics and Divinity, and were to have undertaken a new translation of the Bible, Fagius taking the Old, and Bucer the New Testament. An annual pension of £100 was assigned to each of them, in addition to the salaries they were to receive from the University. However, Fagius did not live a year after reaching England, being attacked by a fever in London and dying at Cambridge November 25, 1549. He was buried in St. Michael's Church, having been, apparently, a member of Trinity College.[1]

Fagius was almost immediately succeeded in the office, which he never filled, by John Immanuel Tremellius. Tremellius, the son of a Jew of Ferrara, was born in that city in 1510. He was converted to the Christian faith, and afterward came in contact with, and accepted ideas of, reformation, especially from Peter Martyr at Lucca. He left Italy with Peter and resided for some time at Strasburg. He came to England some time during the reign of Edward VI, for in April, 1549, he was residing

[1] Cf. Feverlinus, *De vita et meritis Pauli Fagii* (Amsterdam, 1736); also Cooper, *Athenae Cantabrigienses*, II (Cambridge, 1858), 95 ff. The most interesting account of Fagius for the student of Milton is contained in Milton's *The Judgment of Martin Bucer concerning Divorce:* "Paulus Fagius, born in the Palatinate, became most skilful in the Hebrew tongue. Being called to the ministry at Isne, he published many ancient and profitable Hebrew books, being aided in the expense by a senator of that city, ... At length invited to Strasburgh, he there famously discharged the office of a teacher, until the same persecution drove him and Bucer into England, where he was preferred to a professor's place in Cambridge, and soon after died."

with his wife in the household of Cranmer. Before the close of the year he went to Cambridge as lecturer in Hebrew. In 1552 he obtained the grant of a canonry in the church of Carlisle, with a dispensation from residence during the time that he should continue to read Hebrew at Cambridge. In the same month, by the name of Emmanuel Italo, he and his wife, Elizabeth, were made free denizens. He left England at the accession of Mary, and taught Hebrew at Hornbach. He afterward became professor of Hebrew at Heidelberg, removed from there to Metz, and finally to Sedan, at each place teaching Hebrew. He died at Sedan October 9, 1580. The work for which he is best known is the *Biblia Sacra*, which first appeared at Frankfort in 1575. This was the Latin Bible which Milton owned, but in a later edition, after there had been added the New Testament and various other material by the collaboration of Francis Junius.

Both Fagius and Tremellius were men of the profoundest learning, possessed of tremendous continental reputations, the connection of whose names with Cambridge University being of greater significance for the University than for the men themselves. There is preserved a very cogent proof of the respect of the Continent for Tremellius in the way of a letter from Ramus to Tremellius, in which the converted Jew is acclaimed as one of the greatest of living Europeans.[1]

Tremellius was succeeded in the lectureship by Chevalier, who was appointed in 1552 and 1553, and again in 1569. Antoine Rodolphe Chevalier was born in Normandy in 1522–23. He learned Hebrew under Francis

[1] Cf. *Revue Critique*, XV, 295.

Vatablus[1] at Paris, and, being a Protestant, came to England in the reign of Edward. He was favorably known to Fagius and Bucer, the latter recommending him to Cranmer, in whose house he resided for more than a year. He then went to Cambridge, where he gave gratuitous lectures on Hebrew and assisted Tremellius, in whose house he resided and whose step-daughter he married. He was French tutor to the Princess Elizabeth, commonly called "Mr. Anthony" in that connection. He fled from England on the accession of Mary, and was appointed Hebrew professor at Strasburg. From there he went to Geneva, where he taught Hebrew and became acquainted with Calvin. In 1568 he again came to England to solicit the aid of Elizabeth for French Protestants. He read Hebrew lectures at St. Paul's for some time, and was appointed lecturer in Hebrew at Cambridge, as already noted, in 1569. While at Cambridge this second time John Drusius and Hugh Broughton were among his pupils. Broughton says of him: "He was a very learned man, and in Cambridge was accounted second to none in the realm. A rare man he was in that study, and in Hebrew he would draw such a study, that men might learn more of him in a month, than others could teach in ten years." His chief works were a translation from the Aramaic into Latin of the Targum Hierosolymitanum; a Latin version of the Targum of pseudo-Jonathan on the Pentateuch; corrections of the version of Jonathan's Targum on Joshua, Judges, Kings, Isaiah, Jeremiah, Ezekiel, and the twelve minor prophets, all of which were first printed in Walton's Polyglot.

[1] Of Vatablus, Milton remarks in the *Tetrachordon:* "Vatablus within these hundred years professed Hebrew at Paris. . . . ." Apparently Milton knew the Semitic scholars of his time as well as anyone.

Philip Bignon succeeded Chevalier as lecturer, and Cooper says of him:

Philip Bignon, a native of France and probably the son of Francis de Bignon, a French Protestant who fled to England in the reign of Edward VI, read the Hebrew lecture for Mr. Wakefield in and after 1572, being as it is said a member of Corpus Christi College. On Mr. Wakefield's death (1575) Lord Burghley, the Chancellor of the University, recommended Bignon as his successor in the professorship, but the electors could not choose him as he was not a graduate. It does not appear what subsequently became of him.[1]

The professorship for which he unsuccessfully contended was filled by Edward Lively in 1575, immediately upon the death of Wakefield. Lively matriculated at Trinity College in 1564–65, and afterward became a scholar of that house. He graduated B.A. in 1568–69, and became minor fellow of Trinity in 1571 and major fellow in 1572. He himself acknowledged his indebtedness to Whitgift for his training in scholarship. He received his Semitic training from John Drusius.[2] He continued in the Hebrew professorship until his death in 1605.

Lively's successor was Robert Spalding, of whom the best account is contained in Cooper:

[He was] a native of Holderness in Yorkshire, and was matriculated as a sizar of St. John's College in June, 1580, admitted a scholar on Duckett's foundation in 1588, went out B.A. 1588–89, and commenced M.A. 1592. In 1592–93, he was admitted a fellow on Robeby's foundation. He was appointed Hebrew praelector of the college in 1599–1600, again the following year, and once more in 1603–4. In 1600 he proceeded B.D., and was appointed junior dean of St. John's in 1603–4. In compliance with a letter from the King dated Greenwich May 30, 1605, he was elected Regius

[1] Cooper, *op. cit.*, I, 349.   [2] *Ibid.*

Professor of Hebrew (at the death of Lively), which office he held till 1607, when he vacated it, supposedly by death. He was one of the learned men engaged in the translation of the Holy Bible.[1]

In 1608 Andrew Byng was elected to the professorship. There is no need to do more than mention Byng here and note that he was one of the translators of the A.V. and that either he did not prove satisfactory or was himself dissatisfied, as some time near the death of James he was succeeded as professor by Robert Metcalfe, who held the chair until 1648, when he was succeeded by Ralph Cudworth.

Metcalfe apparently did little more than preserve the conventional aspects of the office, even his students, such as Walton and Castell, being unable to make him stand out as a particularly brilliant Semitic scholar, because Semitics at his time was so much further developed at Oxford that such names as Cambridge offers[2] are over-

[1] Cooper, *op. cit.*, II, 479.

[2] Among other eminent men connected with Cambridge *circa* Milton's residence there, the following Semitic scholars are worthy of notice:

Abraham Whelock (1593–1653), graduated B.A., Trinity; M.A., 1618; B.D., Clare, 1625. After election to fellowship he appears to have commenced the study of oriental languages. He both studied and taught Arabic, and was appointed as the first Regius Professor of Arabic in 1633. He published little or nothing, owing, as he says, to the want of Arabic types and compositors capable of setting them up.

Brian Walton (1600–1661), famous as the editor of the Polyglot Bible of 1657 which bears his name, had just left Cambridge as Milton entered.

Edmund Castell (1606–85), almost completely contemporary with Milton, was in residence throughout Milton's Cambridge career. Castell entered Emmanuel College in 1621; B.A., 1624–25; M.A., 1628; and B.D., 1635. He was responsible for the Samaritan, Syriac, Arabic, and Ethiopic versions of Walton's Polyglot. His chief work beside this editing was the *Lexicon Heptaglotton, Hebraicum, Chaldaicum, Syriacum, Samaritanum, Aethiopicum, Arabicum conjunctium, et Persicum separatum*

shadowed by those Oxonians who centered about Lightfoot, Pococke, and Usher.

B.   MILTON AND HIS TUTORS

Such then was the general character of the study of
Hebrew at Cambridge at the time Milton took residence;
it now becomes necessary to turn to his own studies while
there.

Milton's academic work at Cambridge divided itself
into two kinds, the *domi*, or work done within the walls
of his own college, and the *foris*, or the work done in the
University schools. Of the latter, the most important
would have been the listening to lectures by professors
and readers on various and sundry subjects. This would
have been work of a different nature from that he had

(1669), which was an outgrowth of the Polyglot. The man was a perfect
mine of Semitic philology, which was of the nature of its time.

Hackett (*Life of Williams*, p. 10), speaks of one "Rabbi Jacob"
of whom he says: "I remember for a long time a commorant in the University"; he mentions also Robert Spalding, fellow of St. John's and
afterward Regius Professor of Hebrew, and tells us that "with the instruction of these two," William dived far into the mystery of that holy
language (Hebrew)!

John Udall (1560–92) of Trinity College, the poor Puritan who
atoned for his invectives against the bishops by his death in the Marchel-
sea, and whom King James pronounced "the greatest scholar in Europe,"
was the author of a Hebrew grammar. He was a zealous reader of theology,
and developed a strong tendency toward Puritanism while at Cambridge, and also a competent knowledge of Hebrew. In the year following his death there appeared at Leyden a valuable grammar and dictionary of the Hebrew tongue by him under the title: מִפְתֵּחַ לְשׁוֹן הַקֹּדֶשׁ,
that is, *The Key to the Holy Tongue* (Leyden, 1593), 12 mo. The first part
consisted of a Hebrew grammar translated from the Latin of Peter
Martinius; the second part supplied "a practize" or exercises on Psalms
25 and 65, of the nature of those employed by Hoole; while the third
part was a short dictionary of the Hebrew words of the Bible.

done before, and the change must have been a rather difficult one to effect. Just what lectures he attended may
only be guessed at, but probably those on rhetoric, the
languages, and theology would cover the major portion of
such attendance.

The *domi* education would have been much more of a
continuation of the grammar school than was the *foris*,
and in this work he would have been afforded opportunity for guidance in the large amount of reading which
he did as a matter of studying during the seven years he
was in residence. This reading and study would have been
done mostly with tutors, fellows, and other students, and
would have been both a part of, and an addition to, the
reading of ordinary study. He was in this way afforded
ample opportunity to read Latin, Greek, and Hebrew,
together with the modern languages, especially with his
tutor, and would have had opportunity to discuss his readings with other students, tutors, or fellows. Because of
this, the tutors of Christ's in 1625 become important here.

They were, arranged as nearly as possible in the order
of their seniority, William Power, William Siddall, William Chappell, Joseph Meade, John Knowsley, Michael
Honeywood, Francis Cooke, Nathaniel Tovey, Arthur
Scott, Robert Gell, John Alsop, Simpson, and André
Sandelands. All of these were either Bachelors of Divinity or Masters of Arts. That is, all of them were possessed of a more than average linguistic equipment, and,
in the case of the divinity students, a knowledge of Greek
and Hebrew could be assumed, although not depended
upon.

Of these thirteen tutors, but three are of immediate
interest here, which three are William Chappell, Milton's

first tutor; Nathaniel Tovey, who replaced Chappell when Milton returned from rustication; and Joseph Meade.

William Chappell, son of Robert Chappell, was born at Laxton, Nottinghamshire, on December 10, 1582. He was educated in "grammaticals" at Mansfield Grammar School, and when seventeen years of age was sent to Christ's College, Cambridge, where he was elected a scholar. His early career at Cambridge was distinguished above that of his fellows, but want of funds threatened for a time to sever his connections with the University. However, the hope of a fellowship was held out to him, and in 1607 this hope was fulfilled. As a college tutor his fame spread far and wide. "He was remarkable," says Fuller, "for the strictness of his conversation; no tutor in our memory bred more or better pupils,[1] so exact his care in their education. He was a most subtle disputant." Worthington, writing of Meade's habits of discourse, says: "For several years he set apart some of his hours to spend in the conversation of his worthy friend, Mr. William Chappell, who was justly esteemed a rich magazine of Rational Learning."[2]

Chappell had Milton in charge for about a year, having probably been selected as Milton's tutor because of the reputation he had acquired, which was built upon an occurrence which antedated Milton's appearance by about ten years. In the spring of 1615 he had overwhelmed his respondent in a public act of disputation before King James I, when that monarch made his second

[1] It is pertinent to note here that Chappell was tutor in 1617? to John Lightfoot, the greatest Semitic scholar of the seventeenth century.

[2] *The Works of Joseph Mede*, edited by J. Worthington (London, 3d ed., 1672). Author's life.

"visitation" to Cambridge. Chappell is said to have so pressed his opponent that he caused him, Mr. Roberts of Trinity, to faint; whereupon the King himself entered the lists against him, only to be worsted in turn. On the merit thus acquired, for James did not become angry but commended him, Chappell continued a fellow at Christ's for many years. Finally, through Laud's interest, he was transferred in 1633 to the deanery of Cashel in Ireland. Found efficient there in carrying out Laud's views of uniformity, he was promoted to the prevostship of Trinity College, Dublin, and in 1638, to the bishopric of Cork, Clone, and Ross. Had Laud's power lasted longer, Chappel probably would have been awarded an English bishopric, but he was involved in Laud's downfall, left Ireland in 1641, came to England, suffered imprisonment and other indignities during the Civil War, and died at Derby in 1649.

There is no need, and less space, for any discussion here of the many-times-explained rustication episode in connection with Chappell's tutorship of Milton. The relationship between the two was not a happy one, whatever else may have been the conditions which existed for about a year between them. Chappell was too much of a Laudian for a pupil who had been tutored successively by a Young and a Gill. It is the unhappy nature of the relationship which is of significance here, as there are certain aspects of it which throw light on Milton's activities at Cambridge.

Chappell is the third tutor that has been noted, and he is the first of the three with whom Milton has not been in almost perfect amity. Young and Gill were both revered and respected as only teachers who completely gain the confidences of their charges can be revered and respected. Young, as the first tutor, seemed to possess a place apart in Milton's life, and Gill in a measure filled that place when it was left vacant by Young's departure for Holland. It then became evident that Milton needed a tutor who could stand in a very close intimate personal relation to him, and it is worth noting that in the cases of both Young and Gill the outstanding bond appears to have been a linguistic one. In the *Elegia*, Milton eulogizes Young as the one who first introduced him to the "Pierian Spring," and in the first epistle thanks him for the gift of the Hebrew Bible; while in the first epistle to Gill he thanks him for sending the Latin poem, thanks him again for a similar gift in the second epistle, and tells him that he is in turn sending him a translation into Greek hexameters of Psalm 114, which was the Psalm he translated into English verse in the earliest surviving composition of his boyhood. There is present in the Gill epistle, if not the same abounding youthful idolatry of the Young *Elegia*, at least the same measure of respectful friendship and good will which are to be found in the Young correspondence.

With the third tutor, Chappell, no such delightful relationship may be found, for whereas in the cases of Young and Gill relationships became established which were preserved for years, the break with Chappell came but a year after the two met, and was complete. The break was one which must have bitten deep, for when Milton returned to Cambridge, Chappell was no longer his tutor.

Nor was Chappell's successor much more successful in meeting Milton's requirements for a tutor who was at

once guide, counselor and friend. Nathaniel Tovey, born
at Coventry, son of a Mr. Tovey who was master of the
grammar school there, had been taken in charge when
very young by Lucy, Countess of Bedford, who sent him
to Christ's College, Cambridge. Here, after graduating in
Arts, he obtained a fellowship, and in 1621 he held the
Logic Lectureship in the College. Of either his character
or his activities during that period of his life when he was
connected with Cambridge there is no authentic account.[1]
There is little to be said of his relations to Milton, aside
from noting that the Logic Lectureship and the resultant
attention Tovey gave to the subject were undoubtedly of
importance in shaping Milton's attitude toward the subject, and led to the production of the *Artis Logicae*.
Tovey's training leaned heavily toward divinity, though
his Master's degree was in Arts, and Milton might well
have read in the tongues with him as with his predecessor.

But there is entirely lacking in both Chappell and
Tovey what earlier appears to have been an almost essen-
tial requirement for Milton in his tutors, that is, certain
personal traits which would permit of a strong personal
intimacy between pupil and tutor. Tovey, it is true, did
not become the definite antagonist that Chappell did, but
there is no surviving evidence that he, any more than
Chappell, succeeded in becoming a very important figure
in Milton's life.

C.   JOSEPH MEADE AND SEMITIC STUDY

So marked were the traits which bound Milton to
Young and Gill that the absence of those traits in his two
assigned tutors at Cambridge would almost inevitably

[1] Masson, *op. cit.*, I, 130.

lead one to search for the possibility of his having formed
an acquaintanceship and attachment with some other of
the fellows of Christ's. And such a search is not unre-
warded, for there was one among them who embodied in
himself all the necessary characteristics of a Miltonic tutor, including a certain kindliness of manner, a sufficient
breadth of outlook, and a wealth of scholarship which
definitely leaned toward a linguistic emphasis. This fellow was Joseph Mede or Meade, fourth fellow in point of
seniority, but first in point of significance not only for
Christ's, but also for the University, at the time.

While Chappell and Tovey are of interest today almost solely because they were at one time connected, if
only in name, with Milton, Meade was, quite aside from
such possible connection, a rather remarkable figure.
Born in Berden in Essex, in October of 1586, "of Parents
of honest rank," he very early displayed remarkable gifts.
His biographer[1] relates of him:

When he was about ten years old, both he and his father fell
sick at the same time of the small-pox: to the father it proved
mortal, to the son very hazardous. . . . . His mother afterward
married one Mr. Gower, of Nassing in Essex, by whom he was sent
to school, first to Hodsden, and after that to Wethersfield in Essex.
In which time going to London upon some occasion, he bought
Bellarmine's Hebrew Grammar. His master, having no skill in that
language, told him it was not a book fit for him; but he . . . .
would not be discouraged from the perusal of it; but setting upon
it industriously, attained no small skill in the Hebrew tongue before
he left the school.

He was later sent, "because of the pregnancy of his parts,
his assiduous industry, and Proficiency in learning," to
Christ's College, Cambridge, in 1602, with Daniel Rogers

[1] Worthington, *op. cit.* The *Life*, prefaced to the *Works*.

and William Addison as his tutors. He finished M.A. in
1610, and was elected a fellow in 1613. Worthington, his
biographer, continues:

By that time he had taken the degree of Master of Arts he had
made so happy progress through all kind of academical studies, that
it was manifest to all that that title was not (as with too many it is)
any false inscription: He was justly so styled, and was universally
esteemed as one who did well understand all those arts which make
up the accomplishment of a scholar. He was an acute logician, an
accurate Philosopher, a skillful Mathematician, an excellent
Anatomist (being usually sent for when they had any Anatomy in
Caius Colledge), a great Philologer, a master of many Languages,
and a good proficient in the studies of History and Chronology.
. . . . He was chosen fellow of that College upon which the name of
Christ is called. . . . . The fellowship into which he was elected
was that of King Edward's foundation, and therein he was successor to Mr. Hugh Broughton and Mr. Dillingham, both of them
famous for their Hebrew learning; the first abroad, the other at
home, being one of those appointed by Royal Authority to translate
the Bible. . . . . Being thus chosen fellow of the Colledge, he was
not long after made reader of the Greek Lecture of Sir Walter
Mildmay's foundation, and held it all his lifetime: which rendered
that tongue, as also several others, very familiar to him. For his
constant readings upon Homer did not only make him perfect in
that author, but he being a diligent collator of the Greek with
the Hebrew, Chaldee, and Syriac, acquainted himself familiarly
with the idiotisms of all those languages at once. He had besides
made a collection of such Greek, Latine, and English words as he
had observed to have a near sense and sound with the Hebrew; as
we have been informed by some that saw in his study a book of his
in quarto, containing the Hebrew radices with Greek, Latine, and
English words derived from many of them: by which means as
he made the languages more familiar to him, so he consulted the
pleasure and advantage of his friends. . . . . He preserved his
knowledge in Academick learning by the private lectures which he
read to his pupils, to whom he was an able and faithful guide.
For, being a fellow of a Colledge, he esteemed it a part of his duty

to further the education of young scholars; which made him undertake the careful charge of a tutor: and this he managed with great prudence and equal diligence. After he had by daily lectures well grounded his pupils in humanity, logic, and philosophy, and by frequent converse understood to what particular studies their parts might be most profitably applied, he chose rather to set every one his daily task, than constantly to confine himself and them to precise hours for lectures. In the evening they all came to his chamber to satisfie him that they had performed the task he had set for them. The first question which he used to propound to every one in his order was, *Quid dubitas?* What doubts have you met in your studies today? (For he supposed that to doubt nothing and to understand nothing were verifiable alike.) Their doubts being propounded, he resolved their *quaere's*, and so set them upon clear ground to proceed more distinctly: and then having by prayer commended them and their studies to God's protection and blessing, he dismiss'd them to their lodgings. Thus carefully did he discharge the trust of a tutor, though he well knew and was us'd to say that the office of training up young scholars in the university proved oftentimes but a thankless business. In short, he was not for a soft and easie, self-pleasing course of life; but was most willing to spend himself in a laborious endeavoring the best emprovement (not of himself only, but) of others, those especially committed to his care.

He suffered from an impediment in his speech and lacked "that felicity of utterance which useth to set off slight parts, and had so great an hesitation in his speech as rendered his expression painful to himself and less pleasing to others." His early studies disconcerted him to the point of

scepticism, that troublesome and restless disease of the Pyrrhonian school of Old. For lighting upon a book in a neighbor-scholar's chamber (whether it were Sextus Empericus or some other upon the same subject, is not now remembered), he began upon the perusal of it to move strange questions to himself, and even to doubt whether the το Γᾶν, the whole frame of things, as it appears to us, were any more than a mere phantasm or imagination.

Evidently others than Descartes were troubled with doubts at this time. As he cast about for exits from the labyrinth of this "conceit," he delved far "into the most abstruse parts of learning."

Among other studies, he became enmeshed in the study of that medieval chimera, astrology, from which he emerged only after some struggle.

But leaving the hot pursuit of astrological studies (the busy idleness of some even to their old age) he applied himself to the more useful study of history and antiquities, particularly to a curious enquiry into those mysterious sciences which made the ancient Chaldeans, Egyptians and other nations so famous; tracing them as far as he could have any light to guide him, in their Oriental schemes and figurative expressions, as likewise in their hiero-glyphicks, not forgetting to enquire also into the oneirocriticks of the ancients. Which he did the rather because of that affinity which he conceiv'd they might have with the language of the Prophets, to the understanding of whom he shew'd a most ardent desire. His Humanity studies and Mathematical labours were but initial things, which he made attendants to the mysteries of Divin-ity: and thought they were preparatives, as he could use them, yet were they but at a distance off and more remote to his aim; for he had work to do before he could be master of his design. . . . . He was a curious and laborious searcher of antiquities relating to religion, Ethnick, Jewish, Christian, and Mahumetan: the fruits of which studious diligence appear visibly in several of those excellent treatises which have pass'd the press; particularly in his *Apostasie of the Latter Times, The Christian Sacrifice*, his *Discourses upon Daniel*, and other works.

Meade's written work concerned itself almost entirely with biblical exegesis, and he carried this work to a great degree of thoroughness. His greatest work, *Clavis Apo-calyptica*,[1] although of a nature and written on a subject which would be smiled at today, was at the time it was

[1] *Clavis Apocalyptica* (Cambridge, 1627), 4to; 1632, 4to; 1642, 4to.

written a most remarkable and accurate piece of work. Even today, it is recognized, in the rather narrow field in which it belongs, as a definitive examination of many of the problems of interpretation of the Apocalypse. The remainder of his work belongs to another age and another time, when theology more largely determined scholarship than it does now.

His Greek, displayed throughout his writings, was of a very high order of excellence, as befitted an exegetical scholiast, and his Semitic training, although largely of his own founding, was considerable. He employs biblical Hebrew regularly throughout his work, and is never at a loss in scholiazing upon a text or word. The "Chaldee" paraphrase is continually referred to, and both pointed and unpointed quotations from it and rabbinical commentators occur in his writings. His references to the Syriac New Testament involve direct quotation, but the quotation itself is in Latin or Greek or English, the reason for this being that it was almost impossible for Syriac characters to be printed in England at the time he wrote.[1] Hebrew type itself was a problem for the English printer which did not become solved until after 1625,[2] while the Syriac and Arabic were almost unknown as type in England for a long time after Meade's day.[3]

[1] For some of the printing difficulties Semitic scholars were forced to undergo, cf. D. N. B. art., *Edmund Castell* (1606–85); also *Life of William Bedell* (Camden Society, 1872), p. 6.

[2] Cf. Madan, *Early Oxford Press* (Oxford, 1895), p. 126; *Nettles: An Answer to the Jewish Part of Mr. Selden's History of Tithes* (Oxford, 1625). Hebrew pica (unpointed) type is freely used for the first time.

[3] Madan, *op. cit.*, does not record a single printing in Syriac or Arabic type up to 1640, Roman characters being uniformly employed for the purpose.

In addition to these languages, Meade employed the
"Samaritane" Pentateuch, although this Pentateuch was
only accessible since 1616, but, as with Syriac,[1] contented
himself with Latin or Greek translations of the quotations
he used. He also referred to specific books of the Talmud,
so that his range of Semitic reading was, when the entire
list of quotations is considered, extremely large. A man
who could and did use references in Hebrew, pointed and
unpointed, scriptural and rabbinical, pointed and unpointed Aramaic, Syriac, "Samaritane," and who read the
canonical Scriptures, the Targums, the Syriac and Samaritan versions, and the Talmud was, during the first
half of the seventeenth century, little less than a linguistic
giant.

Milton would have come in contact with Meade
through the Greek lectures, and, as during his early years
at Cambridge he was preparing to enter the church, what
more natural than that Meade should have guided the
Semitic study of a student of the college who displayed
the desire to attain competency in the reading of both
Old and New Testaments in their respective originals?
The Greek lectures would have concerned themselves almost wholly with exegesis of the New, and the common
interests of student and lecturer would have supplied
more than enough impetus to the necessary considerations
of the Semitics involved in the study of the Old. Certainly Milton could have found no better guide at Cambridge
for the beginning of serious Semitic study.

[1] On page 232, of the *Works*, occurs an interesting aspect of this
printing difficulty, where he has used unpointed Hebrew characters for
the Syriac, as was done by Tremellius in his edition of 1569, at Geneva.
Cf. *Church Quarterly Review*, XXVI, 257 ff.

V. HORTON AND BEYOND

Almost immediately upon leaving Cambridge Milton retired to, and secluded himself in, his father's estate at Horton, to which the family had moved in 1631. Here was begun that five-year period of lengthened leisure which has come to be known as the Horton period, at once the most regular and pleasing, and hence the best-known period of his life, for, as contrasted with his child-hood and early education, it is fairly well known; it offers no questionably irregular episodes with authority as does the Cambridge period; and there are neither scandalous prose remains nor repellent domestic traditions, as in the later periods. The Horton period attracts alike the casual tyro and the most profound scholar of Miltoniana.

Conventionally treated, the period reeks with that pastoral savor which found poetic expression particularly in *Lycidas*, *Comus*, the *Arcades*, and those two Italianate metrical experiments, *L'Allegro* and *Il Penseroso*, while to it have been allocated nearly all of the more attractive aspects of Milton's peculiar genius. His own statement concerning the period occurs in the *Defensio Secunda*, where he says:

On my father's estate, where he had determined to pass the remainder of his days, I enjoyed an interval of uninterrupted leisure, which I devoted to the perusal of the Greek and Latin classics; though I occasionally visited the metropolis, either for the sake of purchasing books, or of learning something new in mathematics or in music, in which I, at that time, found a source of pleasure and amusement. In this I spent five years, till the death of my mother. . . . .

From this statement it is obvious that (1) the "uninterrupted leisure" meant leisure for study, and (2) that this
study was largely of a linguistic nature centering around
languages and their literatures. Precisely what was read
and studied during this period will never be exactly
known, although the writings of the 1640's are especially
indicative of both the direction and the amount of the
Horton study. Milton himself mentions Greek, Latin,
music, and mathematics, but does not thereby exclude
other interests which, in the light of the writings of the
next ten years, must have absorbed a large amount of the
"uninterrupted leisure." Among such unspecified interests of the Horton period should be placed his interest in
Semitics. This interest, a minor one in comparison with
Latin and Greek, was yet of the same general nature as
these two major interests, being primarily a linguistic interest which led to and supplied a scholarly and literary
intercourse with other minds and opinions.

The year 1641 saw Milton definitely embarked upon
a career of pamphleteering which was to continue for
practically the remainder of his life in varying degrees.
For the ecclesiastical pamphleteering with which he began, he needed the equipment of a cleric, and, according
to his own lights, he had it. He felt himself fitted to employ the patristic theology of the early fathers. Biblical
exegesis, textual criticism of the Hebrew, Greek, or Latin
text of the canon, together with as much ecclesiastical history as he considers necessary, strew the pages of his
pamphlets. The amount of such material is so large that
some opportunity in which to become familiar with the
nature and scope of the field must be postulated in order

to make possible such a sweepingly large range of theological discussion. A considerable linguistic equipment, a large amount of textual and commentary reading, such as the earliest ecclesiastical tracts display, unite in calling for provision for the work which underlies their evidences. When did he do the reading and study which is so much in evidence in the early tracts? Some of it, of course, after the return from Italy; but the backbone of the ecclesiastical tracts was the work done in the Horton period, and to this period I should assign much of the Semitic reading beyond the biblical text of the Hebrew.

The studies of the Horton period were continued after the return from Italy, as the *Divorce Pamphlets* plainly indicate, and the continual appeal in these pamphlets to Hebraic or Semitic authority would further indicate that Milton's Semitic study was probably at its height during the ten years following the return from Italy. This surmise is borne out by the appearance of the *Nine Psalms Done into English Meter* in 1648, the high-water mark of the remaining evidence for Milton's study of the Semitic languages.

The last work in which there is direct evidence of Semitic study having been used for practical and positive furthering of content is in the *Pro Populo Anglicano Defensio*, the work on which he expended the little remaining eyesight he possessed. This work marks the end of direct employment of Semitic study without artistic embellishment, which would indicate that the Semitic field grew not at all for Milton following his blindness, but remained what it had been for him when he was able to browse in it at will. That he never gave up all direct contact with it is attested to by Aubrey, who records of his later years: "After he lost his sight he had a man read to him. The first thing he read was the Hebrew Bible, and that was at 4 h. mane $\frac{1}{2}$ h. (i.e., at 4 A.M., for more than half an hour)."[1]

[1] Aubrey's *Brief Lives*, Clark, II (Oxford, 1898), 68.

CHAPTER THREE
MILTON'S SEMITIC EQUIPMENT

I. THE SEMITIC LANGUAGES WHICH MILTON KNEW AND USED

A. HEBREW

So well known is it that Milton knew and used pointed classic Hebrew that it seems scarcely worth while, other than hastily, again to call attention to the fact. The biographical attestations from Aubrey[1] to Samuel Johnson[2] are so obvious that to mention them is all that is necessary.

There is, however, a basis for the tradition in a biographical fact which has often enough been recognized but never fully examined. This basis is made up of the direct references to Hebrew originals of various biblical passages scattered throughout the prose works. These references have never been carefully examined, and though the immediate results of such examination considered alone are meager, when joined with other pieces of evidence they well repay the labor involved in their examination.

The prose works contain a number of direct references to the Hebrew original of the Old Testament, which, while few in aggregate, are perfectly clear and precise references to Hebrew forms. I now propose to examine the more prominent of these references.

One of the earliest of such references in the prose

[1] Aubrey's *Brief Lives*, Clark, II (Oxford, 1898), 68.

[2] Samuel Johnson, *Life of Milton* in "Lives of the Poets Series" (1780): "He read all the languages which are considered either as learned or Polite: Hebrew, with its two dialects, Greek, Latin, Italian, French, and Spanish."

works occurs in the tractate *The Doctrine and Discipline of Divorce*[1] in this passage:

> The cause of divorce mentioned in the law is translated "some uncleanness," but in the Hebrew it sounds "nakedness of aught, or any real nakedness"; which by all the learned interpreters is referred to the mind as well as the body.

The biblical passage he was discussing is from Deuteronomy 24:1, where the Authorized Version reads: "When a man has taken a wife, and married her, and it come to pass that she find no favor in his eyes, because he hath found some uncleanness in her. . . . ." Milton is here referring to the expression in the Hebrew עֶרְוַת דָּבָר, which expression has been tampered with in the translation, as the marginal rendering of the Authorized Version indicates. The word עֶרְוָה means, as Milton says, "nakedness," as in Genesis 9:22 עֶרְוַת אָבִיו signified "nakedness of his father," while in Genesis 42:9 the expression עֶרְוַת הָאָרֶץ means "nakedness of the land." The fixed expression עֶרְוַת דָּבָר occurs several times in the Old Testament with sufficient flexibility of meaning to permit of the interpretation which Milton gives it; in Deuteronomy 23:15 the expression means "a foul or hateful thing," while in Isaiah 20:4 and I Samuel 20:30 it more nearly conveys the meaning of "disgrace" or "ignominy." It is significant to note in this connection that the Vulgate reading is:

> Si acceperit homo uxorem, et habuerit eam, et non ivenerit gratiam ante oculos eius propter aliquam foeditatem.

[1] I have used a 1645 copy of this work throughout, and it should be noted that this is a reprint of the second, not the first, edition.

Tremellius, the Latin Bible which Milton knew best,[1] read as follows:

Quum ducta quis uxore matitus fuerit eius; fuerit que si non invenit gratiam in oculis illius (quia invenit in ea turpem rem aliquam).

The sense of the flexibility of the expression is indicated in these two Latin versions, and it is evident that Milton had in mind the mutations which the phrase undergoes in the other biblical passages already noted.

The same tractate contains another reference to the original Hebrew of much the same nature. Here Milton says: "And this law the Spirit of God by the mouth of Solomon, Proverbs 30:21–23, testifies to be a good and necessary law, by granting it that a "hateful woman" (for so the Hebrew word signifies, rather than odious, though it come all to one)." The word in question here is שְׂנוּאָה, which is from the root שָׂנֵא, meaning "to hate." The same word, שְׂנוּאָה, occurs again in Deuteronomy 21:15, where the Authorized Version has translated it "hated."

By far the greater number of actual references to, and citations of, the original Hebrew in connection with biblical passages occurs in the *Christian Doctrine*, as would be expected because of the nature of this work, in which Milton deliberately set out with a clearly enunciated guiding principle of analyzing theological doctrine and the Scriptures themselves. He conceived of the bases of such a work as he proposed as made up of these ingredients: "The requisites for the . . . . interpretation of

[1] Cf. Sumner's statement regarding Tremellius Bible in Preface to English translation by Sumner of the *Christian Doctrine*.

Scripture . . . . consist in knowledge of languages; inspection of the originals; examination of the context; care in distinguishing between literal and figurative expressions; . . . . a mutual comparison of texts; and regard to the analogy of faith."

After such a statement as this it is not at all surprising that while in the other prose works there is a tendency to refer to the original Hebrew when citing Old Testament passages, in the *Christian Doctrine* such citation is almost continually to the Hebrew, either by explicit statement or by implication. While these references are so similar in nature to the two already examined as to make specific and separate treatment of them unnecessary, there is a further peculiarity of some of the references in the *Christian Doctrine* that must be noted, which is the citation of the precise Hebrew word or phrase when greater emphasis or more explicit connection is needed than bare references would have supplied.

There are about thirty separate employments of Hebrew word or phrase in the *Christian Doctrine*, each with its elaborate support of concordant passages and parallel usages. Each of these words or phrases is inserted in Hebrew characters, and there are a few peculiarities of the characters and of the masoretic markings which call for some consideration.

Each word or phrase has been used by the author with meticulous care, as relations with the context indicate, such irregularities as occur being due to either the original amanuensis or to the later copyist.

In the original manuscript, to the Columbia photostat of which I shall henceforth refer, the Hebrew begins in very beautiful, almost brush-work, characters, with carefully made and placed vowel points. After the first few, however, the characters become sometimes well made and sometimes almost illegible, with overlappings of the Latin script, as if the Hebrew word or phrase had been inserted after the completion of the Latin text, in spaces purposely left blank. This is especially evident on page 16 of the manuscript, where the Hebrew letter *mem* infringes on the flourish of the "n" of the preceding word, *nomen*.

In many of the words, the accent marks of the Hebrew cantilation have been retained along with the vowel points, indicating that the amanuensis or copyist was reproducing directly from a Hebrew Bible. This is done in the word אֲדֹנָי, on page 13; in אֱלֹהִים, on page 16; in אֲדֹנָיִם, on page 68; in אֲדֹנָי, on page 69, and in בַּעַל, on the same page; in אֲדֹנָי, on page 79; in בָּרָא, on page 114; in בְּרִית, on page 312; in גְּדוּפָה and גֶּהֶם and קְלָלָה and קִלֵּל, on page 561; and in נְשֹׁךְ, on page 681. To offset this, there are the words עַשְׁתָּרֹת, on page 69, and בעל, on page 144, entirely without vowel points, while there also appears on page 69 the word בְּעָלִים insufficiently pointed; but these three words, being proper names—in the order named, Astoreth, Baal, and Baalim—were probably sufficiently well known to the scribe to pass without vowel points. The appearance of the accent marks would indicate the operation of a person who laboriously copied everything in sight in the Hebrew text, but who yet knew enough Hebrew to remember the consonants and appearance of the proper names cited.

However, the employment of Hebrew is accurate, to the point, and everywhere demonstrates Milton's ability to use the pointed text of the Hebrew Scriptures beyond

cavil. More important than this, the continued citation
of Hebraic meanings coupled with the occasional in-
sertion of the actual Hebrew word or phrase can lead to
but one conclusion, which is that Milton, throughout the
Christian Doctrine, and by inference, in his other works,
referred as often to the Hebrew text as to any other version, and always, when the possibility of doubt concerning
a given passage might arise, went direct to the Hebrew
original. This point is important, for it permits the whole
Hebraic canon to operate upon him as a literary influence
during the major portion of his life.

In addition to the two bases already mentioned for
our knowledge of Milton's use of Hebrew, that is, the
biographical tradition and the employment of Hebrew
references in the prose works, there is another basis in
biographical fact which has never been sufficiently in-
vestigated and which is of a greater importance than
either of the other two mentioned because of the implications involved. This is the reference to the Hebrew Bible
in *Epist. Famil. No. 1*, which makes it certain that Milton
actually owned the Hebrew text of Scripture at least as
early as the beginning of his seventeenth year, and accordingly, the pointed text of the Hebrew canon would,
by the time of his blindness, have become almost as
familiar to him as the Latin of Tremellius or the Greek of
the LXX. But no one has ever tried to discover precisely
what this text was or might have been, whereas such a
discovery would be of importance on two counts: first,
that it would be of interest, if only to the curious, to
determine if possible what particular text he actually employed for his Hebrew biblical readings; and secondly, if
the particular text which he is found to have been using

was in any way peculiar, it might be made to yield elements which could be shown to have had some influence upon his writings, whether prose or poetry. However, if only because of the importance as literary influence of the operation upon him of the Hebrew canon, it becomes almost imperative to determine at least one Hebrew biblical text which he used for reading and for reference.

Such a determination would appear to be a hopeless quest upon which to embark, and it would perhaps be even more hopeless were it not for a passage occurring in the *Doctrine and Discipline of Divorce*, commenting upon Judges 19:2, which reads as follows:

> Josephus and the LXX with the Chaldean, interpret only of stubbornness and rebellion against her husband; and to this I add, that Kimchi and two other rabbis who gloss the text, are in the same opinion. Ben Gerson reasons that had it been a whoredom, a Jew and a Levite would have disdained to fetch her again. . . . .

This passage furnishes a good deal of information concerning Milton's biblical reading and his method of biblical interpretation. First of all he has collated the passage with Josephus' *Antiquities of the Jews*, indicating the high value he placed upon Josephus as a secondary authority to Scripture. Next he has used the LXX, and then passed to the Chaldean (Aramaic). The remainder of the quotation, with its reference to Kimchi and two other rabbis "who gloss the text" serves to settle the question of what text he was using, at least as to nature, for there is but one form of text he could have been using to have secured at once the Aramaic interpretation and rabbinical comment. The text to which he was here referring was a rabbinical Bible.[1]

[1] Cf. Thomas Keightley, *An Account of the Life, Opinions, and Writings of John Milton* (London, 1855), p. 243.

Now a rabbinical Bible is a peculiarly constructed work. It contains in the central interior of its necessarily immense pages parallel columns of text, in one the classic pointed Hebrew of the Torah, and in the other, the Targum, or Aramaic paraphrase of the Hebrew text. These two textual columns are surrounded usually completely, by the commentary, which has gradually become attached to the text. This commentary is known as the Masorah magna or the Masorah parva, according as it graces the sides or the top and bottom of the textual columns. It was in these Masorah that Milton found the interpretations of Kimchi and the other rabbis, and his mention of Ben Gerson should make it possible to establish the identity of the particular rabbinical Bible he was using.

The *Doctrine and Discipline of Divorce* was written about 1640, and at that time the number of printed rabbinic text editions was small. The first printed rabbinic Bible was the famous Bomberg edition, published at Basle in 1517 and edited by Felix Pratensis. This edition was not pleasing to the Jews of Europe, perhaps because its editor was a convert to Christianity, and it was replaced in 1525 by the second Bomberg text, which more than any other influenced all later texts. In 1546–48 appeared a third edition of the Bomberg rabbinic Bible, which was practically a reprint of the second, with some changes in the Masorah. This third edition was repeated in the fourth edition of Treves, and the fifth was a reprint of the second. The sixth edition was edited by Johann Buxtorf (Buxtorf I) and published by him at Basle in 1618–19.[1] This edition was a reprint of the edition of 1546–48 and

---

[1] The copy in the library of the University of Michigan is dated 1620.

became widely circulated among Gentiles in Europe because Buxtorf himself was widely known.

This Buxtorf edition became the most readily obtainable of all rabbinic Bibles. It was three years in the making, and its advent widely anticipated and discussed because of the almost universal use of Buxtorf's grammar,[1] first published in 1605. It is at least significant that the date of the Buxtorf edition (*ca.* 1620) and the date of Milton's *Epist. Famil. No. 1* (1625) are sufficiently close together to warrant the conjecture that it may have been for the receipt of a copy of the Buxtorf Bible that Milton was thanking Young in that epistle.

However, the commentators on Judges 19:2 whom Milton mentions afford sufficient basis for the determination of the source he was using. He adds to Josephus, the LXX, and the Aramaic Targum, "Kimchi and two other rabbis who gloss the text" to support the particular contention he is securing from the verse cited. His number of commentators is the same as the number of commentators on the verse in the Buxtorf Bible, for in Buxtorf three and precisely three comment on this verse. One of the three is Kimchi, רדק, whom Milton explicitly mentions. Another is Rashi, רשי, whom Milton does not mention by name. The third is Ben Gerson, רלבג, who contributes by far the longest comment and whom Milton specifically quotes. His quotation of Gerson is like most Miltonic quotations in that it is a quotation which is made to serve the purpose at hand, as a citation of Gerson will show. Gerson says:

[1] *Praeceptiones Grammaticae de Lingua Hebraea* (Basle, 1605).

וספר עוד כי בימים ההם שלא היה מלך
בישראל שיוכיח החוטאים חית איש לוי גר
בירכתי אפרם ולקח לו אשה פלגש מבית
לחם יהודה וזנתה עליו פלגשו ר͏ל שנטתה
ממנו ושבה אל בית אביה לברוח ממנו וזה
היה הזנות הזה כי הנטייה איך שתחיה תקרא
זנות אמר זנותיין ותירוש יקח לב והוכרחנו
לפרש הענין בזה האופן שאם זנתה עליו
לשכב עם זולת אישה היתה אסור לבעלה
ולא היה ראוי שישוב לבקשה עוד אבל
ענין זנותה ביאר במה שאמר ותלד
מאתו אל בית אביה שעמדה שם זמן
ארוך כמו שביאר שעמדה שם שנה
וארבעה חדשים וזה ממה שהודה
שאין וכובה לשוב אליו עוד והיה ובותינו
ז͏ל פירשו וכשראה זה אישה הלך אחרה
לדבר על לבה להשיבה כי ידמה שסרה
ממנו על דבר הקטטות שהקניטה בביתו
יͯול זה לפיסה ובזה האזפן הלך להשיבה

---

[1] The characters of the rabbinic text are here transcribed into regular
Hebrew characters; otherwise no changes have been made. I am indebted to Professor Leroy Waterman of the University of Michigan for
this translation:

"And the book adds that in those days, when there was no king in
Israel, the challenger of transgressors, there was a man, a Levite, a
sojourner who dwelt on the outlying slopes of Ephraim. And this man
took to himself a wife, a concubine from Beth-Lehem Judah. And she
committed adultery against him (RL) in that she turned from him and
returned to the house of her father to escape from her husband. And as
for this adultery, it was because of turning from him that it was called
adultery. Adultery is like [literally is called] wine and *must*, which take

Milton has taken this to mean that had the woman actually committed the carnal act which the Hebrew text specifies, Ben Gerson would never have gone to the trouble to explain at such length why the woman's defection was not the usual crime of adultery, else a Jew and a Levite would never have gone "to fetch her again," as he actually did go.

There can be no question that Milton was here making direct usage of the Masorah of a rabbincal Bible, which inevitably means that he was reading the peculiar unpointed rabbinic jargon of the margins. This is most significant, for it opens to him almost every rabbinic, masoretic, or medieval work printed before 1650 or before his blindness.[1] Much of this material cannot be particularly connected with England, but Milton's continental journey provides a means of contact with printed rabbinic literature which would have been sufficient, while the mass of material contained in the printed Masorah of

---

away the understanding and make it difficult to distinguish a matter, for if she committed adultery against him, it was only in lying apart from him, and it has not been sufficiently emphasized that he went to seek her again in spite of the matter of her so-called "adultery," which is thereby explained. It is said that she went from him to the house of her father and remained there for a long time, and this is further explained by the fact that she remained there a year and four months. This shows that she had no inclination to return to him again, but he had many [i.e., to return to her]. (L) This is the explanation that when her husband saw this, he went after her to speak to her heart and to bring her back again when he had become calm, for she vexed him in his house and because of this he became displeased with her [literally, "caused her to hide her face"] and this is the reason why he went to bring her back."

[1] The reference to Kimchi and Ben Gerson was in the first (1643) edition of the *Doctrine and Discipline of Divorce*, and was of course retained in subsequent editions.

the Buxtorf Bible alone makes this connection of Milton with a rabbinic Bible of tremendous importance.

B.   ARAMAIC (CHALDEE)

The statement by Edward Phillips concerning the Semitic training to which he and his brother were submitted during the time that Milton was charged with their education is the prime external source for Milton's knowledge and use of Aramaic or Chaldee. Phillips says:

> Nor did the time thus studiously employed in conquering the Greek and Latin tongues hinder the attaining to the chief Oriental languages, viz., the Hebrew, the Chaldee, and Syriac, so far as to go through the Pentateuch, or Five Books of Moses in Hebrew, to make a good entrance into the Targum or Chaldee Paraphrase, and to understand several chapters of St. Matthew in the Syriac Testament.

Besides this statement, there is Milton's own on the same subject in the tractate *Of Education:*

> Ere this time the Hebrew tongue at a set hour might have been gained, that the Scriptures may now be read in their own original; whereto it would be no impossibility to add the Chaldee, and the Syriac dialect.

The incentive for the acquisition of Aramaic or Chaldee was of course to be able to read the Targums or paraphrase in a later dialect of the Hebrew canonical text, and direct evidence for such reading occurs in a passage in the *Apology for Smectymnuus:*

> Omitting that place in Numbers at the killing of Zimri and Cozbi, done by Phineas in the height of zeal, (Num. 25:7) related, as the rabbins expound, not without an obscene word, we may find in Deuteronomy and three of the prophets, where God, denouncing bitterly the punishments of idolaters, tells them in a term im-

modest to be uttered in cold blood, that their wives shall be openly defiled. But these, they will say, were honest words in that age when they were spoken. Which is more than any rabbin can prove; and certainly had God been so minded, he could have picked such words as should have come into abuse. What will they say to this? . . . . Turn then to the first of Kings (1 Kings 14:10) where God himself uses the phrase. . . . . Which had it been an unseemly speech in the heat of an earnest expression, then we must conclude that Jonathan or Onkelos the targumists were of cleaner language than he that made the tongue; for they render it briefly, "I will cut off all who are at years of discretion. . . . ."

He was here comparing the reading of the Hebrew text with the reading of the Aramaic paraphrase or of the Targum for that particular textual passage. The Hebrew here is וְהִכְרַתִּי לְיָרָבְעָם מַשְׁתִּין בְּקִיר. This reading has been retained in the Vulgate, which reads, *et percutiam de Ieroboam mingentem ad parietem*. The Latin *mingentem* exactly translates, so far as meaning is concerned, the Hebrew מַשְׁתִּין. But the Targum reads וְאֲשֵׁצֵי לְיָרָבְעָם יָדַע מַדָּע. And in this, as Milton has stated, the whole offensive phraseology of the original has been eliminated.

C. RABBINICAL HEBREW

The third Semitic dialect with which Milton was familiar was that peculiar jargon in which the Masorah were written, the language of the marginal commentary of the rabbinical Bible. This dialect was a strange mixture of Hebrew and Aramaic, which, while formidable, would have presented but few difficulties to Milton, who could read both Hebrew and Chaldee. He refers to its employment in the passages already quoted and in many others in the prose writings.

D. SYRIAC

As with Aramaic, Edward Phillips forms the basis for recorded knowledge of Milton's Syriac. In the passage previously quoted from Phillips' *Life of Milton*, Phillips says that Milton required him and his brother to read the Gospel of Matthew in Syriac, from the Syriac Testament. This was probably Tremellius' edition, published at Paris in 1569 and well known in England since its first appearance in the sixteenth century.

Milton has left many evidences of his employment of Syriac collations which, beside his suggestion to include Syriac in his projected curriculum in the tract *Of Education*, constitute very obvious reasons for including Syriac in any summation of his Semitic equipment. As early as the *Tetracordon* of 1644–45 occurs an instance of collation with the Syriac text which is most interesting in its implications. In calling attention to the question which the Pharisees asked of Jesus: "Is it lawful for a man to put away his wife for every cause"?, Milton says of the phrase, "for every cause," "The Syriac translator renders it conformably upon any occasion or pretense." The point made is very slight, yet the collation directly with the Syriac is important. This confirms Phillips' statement relative to the reading of the Gospel of Matthew in Syriac, for the passage in question is taken from Matthew 19:3–4, in which passage the Vulgate reading for this phrase is *quacumque ex causa*, while that of the Syriac is *ex qualibet occasione*[1]

Another almost equally early reference to the Syriac occurs in the *Areopagitica* (1644): "As for the burning

---

[1] I have used the Latin paraphrase of Brian Walton's Polyglot Bible (London, 1654), for the translation of Syriac passages.

of those Ephesian books by St. Paul's converts, it is replied, the books were magic, the Syriac so renders them." And so it does, amplifying the Vulgate, which was followed by the Authorized Version in this verse (Acts 19:19): "Many of them also . . . . brought their books together and burned them." The Syriac reads: *multi magi congregarunt libros suos, allatosque concremarunt.*

The largest number of references to Syriac renderings of Scripture occurs, as would be expected, in the posthumous *Christian Doctrine*, in which work, as was found to be true of the employment of Hebrew references, there are many actual references to the Syriac, and many more, perhaps, inferred. All of them which are specific are of a similar nature to the two which have been considered and need not be examined in detail. There are at least a dozen definite references to the Syriac version of the New Testament and as many more indefinite ones, so that Milton's knowledge of at least New Testament Syriac becomes very firmly established.

E. OTHER SEMITIC LANGUAGES

There are two other possibilities to be added to the list of Semitic languages Milton knew, although they hardly emerge as more than possibilities, but the nature of the evidence makes it necessary to include a discussion of them.

In that chapter of the *Christian Doctrine* entitled "On the Son of God," Milton discusses the nature of the relationship of the Son and the Father and, as is well known, reaches an anti-trinitarian position. One of the means by which he arrives at his ultimate position is the citation of scriptural passages. In the intensity of his discussion of the Trinity he of course could not overlook I John 5:7: "For there are three that bear record in heaven, the Father, the Word, and the Holy Ghost: and these three are one." The manner in which he succeeds, to his own satisfaction, in circumventing this obstacle is at once curious and, for present purposes, highly informative. He says, after having quoted the accepted reading, "But not to mention that this verse is wanting in the Syriac and the other two Oriental versions, the Arabic and the Ethiopic, as well as in the greater part of the ancient Greek MSS, and that in those which actually contain it, many various readings occur." This quotation raises a rather pointed question: How, and in what form, did Milton know of Arabic and Ethiopic versions of the New Testament? Is this passage an indication that he knew and read these two languages, or at least those portions of the scriptural fragments which were then available in these two languages? And if he did, what was the form in which he knew either the fragments or the languages? Was his Semitic learning of an even broader nature than has ever been hinted?

Unfortunately for the alluring possibilities raised by such conjectures, other facts must be considered which rudely jolt the possibility of such a tremendous scope for his Semitic equipment, for, in the first place, this is the sole direct reference to either of the two dialects, Arabic or Ethiopic, to be found anywhere in his works, and unlike the Hebrew, Chaldee, or Syriac, there is for them no external evidence supplied by a Phillips or anyone else. Without such confirmatory evidence existing, the burden of proof for the implications of this particular passage must be borne by the passage itself, and a full consideration of it yields only negative results. Milton was, in this passage, literally moving heaven and earth in order to make his point, and, in his all but omnipotent maneuvering employing everything which swam within his ken to secure the interpretation he required. He already was acquainted with the Syriac New Testament, in which, as he rightly says, the seventh verse of the fifth chapter of I John, and all of II and III John, for that matter, are wanting. The checking of the Syriac omission would probably have exhausted his ability to check directly the various versions of this passage. However, there is a very significant aspect of the names and number of versions which he cites, which are the Latin Tremellius—he was writing in Latin and the Latin quotation confirms the reading of Tremellius rather than that of the Vulgate[1]— the Greek, of which he mentions, without directly naming, several manuscripts; the Syriac; the Arabic; and the Ethiopic; or five specific versions. Of the Latin and the Greek, it is significant to note that in the canonical reading of Tremellius, from Beza, which is paralleled by Tremellius' own translation of the Syriac with verse 7 lacking, there is a marginal note of the canonical verse which reads as follows:

Totum septimum versiculum Syrum Testamentum omittet, sicut etiam multi Graeci codices, qui ita restitui posset,

וחלהא אנון רסחרין בשמיא אבא מלתא
ודוחא קרישא ותל תחון חר אנון

[1] Vulgate (1654), I John 5:7: "Quonam tres sunt qui testimonium dant in coelo: Pater, Verbum, et Spiritus sanctus; et hi tres unum sunt." Tremellius (1617), *ibid.*: "Nam tres sunt qui testificantur in caelo, Pater, Sermo, et Spiritus sanctus; et hi tres unum sunt." Milton, *Doctrina Christiana*: "Tres sunt qui testificantur in coelo, Pater, Sermo, et Spiritus sanctus, et hi tres unum sunt."

id est. Nam tres sunt, etc. Sed quia non modò in impresso, sed etiam in manuscripto codice Heidelbergensi omittebatur, nec in omnibus vetustis Graecis codicibus legebatur, textui inserere non sum ausus: ne tamen versiculorum fieret perturbatio, utque eorum numeri responderent numeris versiculorum Graeci textus, a sexto translii ad octavum.

This note of Tremellius might well have been, and probably was, the authority for Milton's statement relative to the non-appearance in many, and confusion in all, of the Greek manuscripts of the verse; but Tremellius furnishes no clue to the Arabic or Ethiopic.

However, the number and names of the versions cited by Milton offer a possible solution, together with the conjectural dating of the *Christian Doctrine* in the late fifties, the most carefully determined date being about 1657.[1] The problem of the acquaintanceship with the Arabic and Ethiopic resolves itself therefore into a question of what possibility there was at about that date, 1657, for access to such versions? The answer to this is not far to seek, for Brian Walton's famous Polyglot Bible appeared in 1654, and it is particularly significant that this work contained exactly the same number of versions of exactly the same names for I John as Milton mentioned, viz., the Vulgate or Latin, the Septuagint, the Syriac, the Arabic, and the Ethiopic, and that the seventh verse of the fifth chapter of the first Johannine epistle is wanting in the Syriac, in the Arabic, and in the Ethiopic versions there given. In other words, Milton, in being so precise in his collation of this verse, has listed exactly the versions which Walton included for this epistle, and it seems to me more than a presumption that this Bible of

[1] J. H. Hanford, "The Date of the Christian Doctrine," *Studies in Philology*, XVII, 309 ff.

Walton lay before Milton and his amanuensis when the passage in the *Christian Doctrine* was being written.

Not a great amount of credence, therefore, can be given to the hypothesis that Milton knew Arabic and Ethiopic, although not even such a coincidence as has just been pointed out can entirely exclude the possibility of his having known them. But on the basis of the only evidence as yet known, and that as questionable as it has been found to be, any such assumption for the present must be negative.

II. MILTON'S KNOWLEDGE OF
SEMITIC LITERATURE

A. THE HEBREW CANON

As I have already pointed out, Milton was, from 1625 onward, familiar with the canon of the Hebrew Scriptures in their original, and if the Hebrew Bible sent him by Young was the rabbinical Bible which he is later found using, he must have been very well acquainted with the three tongues to be found therein.

The implications of his having known the Hebrew and Aramaic versions of the Old Testament are of importance in any consideration of his employment of Scripture, as it may be assumed that in all of his references to the Old Testament he was referring to, and using whenever desirable, the Hebrew original. Important as such a consideration may be, it is of far less literary importance than the possibilities which arise from the mine of material imbedded in the rabbinical comment which littered the margins of whatever rabbinic text he was using. I have assumed that this text was the Buxtorf Bible; but even if it had been some other rabbinical edition, the Masorah would have been the same. This rabbinical comment would have opened to him all the medieval Jewish comment and writing of almost every conceivable nature, for after all it had but one fundamental aspect, which was some phase of biblical interpretation.

B. THE TALMUD

In the long tractate, *Pro Populo Anglicano Defensio*, occurs a reference to the Talmud which, so far as I am aware, has never been adequately explained. Numerous oblique references to this huge Hebraic compilation occur elsewhere in the prose, but this particular reference is of a much more direct nature than any of the others and soon proves itself to be of great significance.

Milton is busily refuting Salmasius' points of scriptural support of monarchy and divine right of kings when he suddenly, in answer to Salmasius' suggestion, throws out the following:

> Then you come to the rabbins and quote two of them, but you have as bad luck with them here as you had before. For it is plain, that that other chapter that Rabbi Joses speaks of and which contains, he says, the right of kings, is that in Deuteronomy, and not in Samuel. For Rabbi Judah says very truly, and against you, that that discourse of Samuel's was intended only to frighten the people.

In this passage Milton is referring very clearly to the Babylonian Talmud, for the discussion of the right of kings to which he refers occurs in the Gemara to the third Mishna of the Sanhedrin tractate, and is as follows:

> According to R. Jose, all that is written concerning a king in Samuel, the king is allowed to do. R. Jehudah, however, *maintains on the basis of Deuteronomy 17:15 that the whole portion is written only to frighten them* [i.e., the people], *as the expression in Deuteronomy means that the fear of the king shall always be upon you.*[1]

This reference establishes beyond question that Milton knew at least this portion, the Tractate Sanhedrin, of the Talmud, although the question of the exact form in which he knew it cannot be answered on the basis of this or any other of his references to it. But so far as the literary effect of his reading of this work is concerned, it makes

[1] M. L. Rodkinson, *Babylonian Talmud*, VII-VIII (New York, 1902), p. 52, Sec. 'Jurisprudence, [Damages] Tract Sanhedrin."

very little difference whether he read it in its original
form, in Latin translation, or in English, and I am perfectly willing to grant the possibility of any one of these
or of all three, for the most important aspect of the
establishment of his contact with this work lies in the
influence the material contained therein would have had
upon his literary productions.

C. SEMITIC BIBLICAL TEXTS

A complete list of the Semitic biblical texts which
Milton mentions in such a manner as to identify them are
the Hebrew, the Aramaic, the Syriac, the Arabic, and the
Ethiopian. In the previous discussion of these last two
versions or texts, the probability of his having known
them by means of Walton's Polyglot Bible was pointed
out, and this Bible would have been a means by which
he may have known other texts than those already mentioned.

This immense work, in some ways the finest flower of
all English scholarship, was, so far as the labor of its
editing was concerned, the result of the operations of the
man whose name it bears, Brian Walton (1600–1661).
Walton was born at Seymour, in the district of Cleveland,
Yorkshire. He went to Cambridge as a sizar of Mag-
dalene College in 1616, migrated to Peterhouse in 1618,
and there proceeded B.A. in 1619, and M.A. in 1623, two
years before Milton went to Cambridge. After holding a
schoolmastership and two curacies, he was made rector
of St. Martin's Orgar in London in 1628. He was connected with the controversy between citizens and the
London clergy about the city tithes, and compiled a
treatise on the subject. This treatise was remembered in

1641, and articles were brought against him in Parliament, which appear to have led to the sequestration of his very considerable preferments. He was also charged with popish practices, and in 1642 he was ordered into custody as a delinquent, whereupon he took refuge in Oxford and ultimately returned to London more or less secretly to the house of William Fuller (1580?-1659), dean of Ely, whose daughter, Jane, was his second wife. In and during his retirement he gave himself largely to oriental studies, and planned and carried through his great project, the Polyglot Bible, which bears his name. He intended that this work should be more complete, cheaper, and provided with a better critical apparatus than any previous work of the kind. His first proposals for the Polyglot appeared in 1652, and the work itself appeared in six large folios in 1657, having been printing for five years. Nine languages were used for the texts and versions, although never more than five versions of the same passage of Scripture appear at the same time. The languages of the various versions were Hebrew, Chaldee, or Aramaic, Samaritan, Syriac, Arabic, Persian, Ethiopic, Greek, and Latin. Each of the versions, except the Vulgate, of course, was accompanied by a Latin translation or paraphrase, in the case of the Hebrew text, the Latin being an interlinear verbatim translation.

Walton himself was not, as the title but not the contents would indicate, responsible for either text or translation, having acted more as an editorial prime mover in the project. Among his many collaborators were James Usher, John Lightfoot—whom many scholars have styled the greatest Semitic scholar the English-speaking world has produced—Edward Pococke, Edmund

Castell, whose *Lexicon Heptaglotta* of 1669 was an outgrowth of the Polyglot, Abraham Whelocke, Patrick Young, Thomas Hyde, and Thomas Graves. Many of these names are at once recognizable as those of translators of the Authorized Version, and in fact this Bible was in reality a belated effect of the Authorized Version upon English scholarship.

The great undertaking was liberally supported by subscription, and Walton's political opinions did not deprive him of the help of the Commonwealth and the interest of Cromwell. The paper upon which the work was printed, necessarily imported, was free from duty, and Cromwell's interest was acknowledged in the original Preface, part of which was afterward canceled to make way for more loyal expressions toward the restored monarchy, under which oriental studies immediately began to languish.

Without more evidence than is as yet available, it is idle to speculate as to whether Milton read all of the versions contained in the Polyglot. I would suggest that the many visitors of the blind Latin secretary of the 1650's may well have comprised individuals who could have read any or all of the various versions with which there was the possibility of unfamiliarity to Milton, in a manner which would have supplied him with the nature of versional variations from the texts he already knew so well. But the entire matter awaits more specific evidence.

D. THE CAMBRIDGE SEMITIC SUCCESSION

As noted in an earlier chapter, Milton displayed a peculiar interest in, and knowledge of, sixteenth-century

Semitic scholars, especially those connected with Cambridge. As I have pointed out elsewhere, he definitely mentioned Martin Bucer, Paulus Fagius, Tremellius, and the famous French translator of the Bible, Vatablus. Each of these scholars, provided that he knew their works—and Milton's mere mention of an author usually implies that—would have taken him a long way into Semitic scholarship and Semitic reading.

Martin Bucer (1491–1551) was certainly known to Milton, as he anonymously published *The Judgment of Martin Bucer Concerning Divorce* in 1644. Most of Bucer's work was concerned with the New Testament, but he published *Sacrorum psalmorum libri quinque, ad Ebraicam veritatem traducti* at Strasburg in 1529, *Commentarii in librum Judicum* at Paris in 1554, *Commentaria in librum Job* in 1528, and *in Ecclesiasticen* in 1532.

Paulus Fagius (1504–49), who accompanied Bucer to Cambridge in the year in which he died, was more nearly a pure Semitic scholar than was Bucer. Much of the Latin translation of the Aramaic of the Walton Polyglot was done by Fagius, while practically all of his work was translation of text, paraphrase, or commentary of the Old Testament. Acquaintanceship with such an author would have led Milton very far into the mazes of Semitic scholarship in so far as that scholarship centered itself upon Scripture. Text, Targum, and rabbinical comment would have been spread out before him in tremendously large quantities, with all of the perspicuity of as fine a critical mind as any Gentile ever brought to bear upon Hebraic literature or commentary operating continuously upon the mass of material with which Fagius worked. Contact with the work of Fagius would imply that whatever the quantity of Semitic learning Milton himself possessed, the quality of that learning would have been of the highest order, and in his high praise of Fagius and his work he exhibits that uncanny characteristic of his— the ability to pierce through almost unerringly to the soundest authority, to align himself almost inevitably with the most permanent activities in any given field, and to hold to them, sometimes in the face of contrary contemporary opinion.

So, with Tremellius, Milton selected the other most considerable Semitic scholar of the gentile and Protestant world. Tremellius was an even more broadly ranging worker than Fagius, and included among his many activities the editing and translating of more Semitic dialects than did Fagius. Knowing the two of them, Milton would have possessed more than an ordinary littérateur's share of a knowledge of the entire field of Semitic scholarship as it then existed.

The mention of Vatablus serves as an indication that the field of biblical translation was particularly well known and familiar to him, for with Vatablus mentioned, Milton is now known to have been familiar with the translation of the Bible into the three most important languages of his time: the English, the Italian of Diodati, and the French of Vatablus.

With the cessation of the stream of continental Semitic scholars to Cambridge, there was no particular distinction connected with the succeeding scholars until the time of Ralph Cudworth, so that Milton's failure to mention any of the later succession is indicative of a silence due to the mediocrity of the material rather than to any diminution in his interest in the subject.

E. JOHN SELDEN

That this writer was known to Milton is attested by two entries in the *Common-place Book*, Nos. 70 and 76, as well as by several references to him in the prose. Selden, who was primarily a barrister who refused to have much to do with the practical considerations of a lawyer's life but insisted upon engaging himself as, and with what, he pleased, very early turned his prodigious intellect to the pursuit of oriental studies, with the result that he produced three works which with remarkable success have withstood the test of time. His *De Juri Naturali et Gentium juxta Disciplinam Hebraeorum* (1640), *Uxor Ebraica* (1646), and *De Diis Syris* (1617), carried him far into the realm of Semitic scholarship. These major works, as well as the minor *De successionibus in bona defunctorum ad leges Ebraeorum* (1631) and *De Synedriis Veterum Ebraeorum* (1650) consisted mainly in the exposition of Jewish or rabbinical law, and perhaps no Englishman ever went farther in this field than did Selden.

CHAPTER FOUR

THE APPEARANCE OF SEMITIC MATERIAL
IN MILTON'S POETRY

I. THE EARLY POETRY AND THE TRANSLATIONS OF THE PSALMS

Except as the poems written before 1641 give some slight indications of Semitic, or at least oriental, readings, they furnish very few evidences of Semitic influences. There is a reference in *Il Penseroso* to "thrice great Hermes," an echo from the Latin exercise *De Idea Platonica* of Cambridge days, and no more than that. But other than this there is little or nothing of such a nature as to indicate a definite Semitic origin, and on the basis of these early poems alone, almost nothing could be predicated as regards a specific Semitic influence.

The translations of the Psalms of 1648, on the other hand, offer a peculiar insight into the nature of Milton's Semitic scholarship and its influence on his work. By means of them there is to be gained an idea of how Milton worked before his blindness came to him, and such an idea as none of his other poetry supplies of the workings at the same time of the scholarly and poetical phases of his complex nature.

In the preface to these translations he boldly proclaimed, "Nine of the Psalms done into metre; where in all, but what is in a different character, are the very words of the Text, translated from the original." It is clear from this statement that he set himself the task of, first, reproducing the Psalms in English verse, and secondly, presenting a literally faithful translation with properly indicated departures from the original. In the edition of 1673, to which I shall hereafter refer, such departures are in italics, as they are in most subsequent editions of these Psalms.

The task which Milton set himself was therefore twofold, and one which called into play at once the skill of the translator and the art of the poet. Baldwin has called attention to some apparent discrepancies in the translation;[1] one might more appropriately call attention to the uniformly mediocre character of the poetry, for the difficulty in both cases lies in the nature of the task assumed.

Close examination of the original Hebrew of the Psalms he used and Milton's version gives rise to two qualitatively different questions, which only the results of such examination can answer: Shall apparent swervings from the Hebrew original be accepted as indicative of Milton's lack of thoroughgoing Semitic scholarship, or was his scholarship adequate enough, but his poetic ability unequal to the task of at once remaining literal and artistic?

If the Hebrew original be translated with care, and then such translation be compared with Milton's version, certain striking peculiarities of the Miltonic version will become apparent which will cause some readjustment of the whole conception of the importance of the Psalms translations, so that they will gain in significance as indicators of Milton's Semitic scholarship and lose in significance as indicators of his poetic ability.

It is well at this point to remember that Milton had been working with the Psalms, reading them, paraphrasing them, translating them into and from Latin, Greek, Italian, English, and Hebrew since his early school days.

---

[1] E. C. Baldwin, "Milton and the Psalms," *Modern Philology*, XVII, 457 ff.

The earliest of his poems preserved is the Psalm 114, paraphrased from an English version, probably. If, as Masson surmised,[1] not without some warrant, it seems to me, that the stimulant for these experimentations with metrical translations was the then current controversy over a new version of the Psalms for use in public worship, then the very form in which he rendered these translations would inevitably point to a continual comparison with other metrical versions he knew, as in any competitive exercise, and so with any and all versions, metrical or otherwise, with which he was familiar. Even though he had had no intention of engaging in the controversy, the many versions which he seems to have known would still have exerted their influences upon his work, especially in the minor details of the composition. Moreover, the effects of these other versions upon him would have been cumulative and need not have been specifically and consciously present in his mind while he was composing his own verse forms.

In order to answer the two questions which have arisen regarding the relation of Milton's scholarship and poetic ability, it will be necessary to examine in detail his translations and the Hebrew original, although it will be scarcely necessary to consider in this way the complete translation of the entire group of nine Psalms in order to discover the trend of such a comparison in connection with the questions already raised. In this connection the analysis of a single Psalm (Psalm 82) will suffice in supplying an instance of what actually took place in these translations.

[1] David Masson, *The Poetical Works of John Milton*, I (London, 1896), 77.

The first verse of this Psalm Milton has translated thus:

> God in the great assembly stands
> *Of kings and lordly states;*
> Among the gods on both his hands
> He judges and debates.

The Hebrew for this verse is:

אֱלֹהִים נִצָּב בַּעֲדַת־אֵל בְּקֶרֶב אֱלֹהִים יִשְׁפֹּט

This, literally translated, is:

> God (Elohim) stands ("in the sense of
> taking one's stand") in (the)
> assembly of God (mighty) in midst of gods
> he will judge.

Milton's whole second line is in italics, a confessed interpolation, and the two verbs in the last line are from the single יִשְׁפֹּט in the Hebrew. Here is apparently a deviation from the original, which, though indicated by italics, is yet hardly defensible, for he seems to have confused the assembly of gods with an assembly of gods and kings or potentates. The Vulgate clearly does not permit this:

> Deus stetit in synagoga deorum: in medio
> autem deos diiudicat.

Tremellius, however, more nearly renders the Hebrew, and in his *magistratus* there is a suggestion of "kings and lordly states":

> Deus astat in coetu Dei fortis, inter
> magistratus iudicat.

This is very similar to Walton's paraphrase of the Hebrew:

> Deus stans in coetu fortis, in interiori
> divorum judicabit.

Walton's paraphrase of the Targum is curious and to the point:

> Deus cujus magestas commoratur in congregatione
> justorum qui potentes sunt in Lege: in medio
> judicum *veritatis* judicat.

The Syriac takes an entirely different tack:

> Deus stetit inter coetum angelorum, et in medio
> Angelorum judicabit.

Diodati's Italian translation, which Milton knew very well,[1] follows the Vulgate:

> Iddio e presente nella raunanza di Dio: egli
> giudica nel mezzo degl'iddij.

In the English translations and in Latin and in English metrical versions two interpretations manifest themselves. In the Coverdale Bible of 1535, the verse reads thus:

> God stondeth in the congregacion of the goddes,
> & is a iudge amonge the iudges.

In the Great Bible of 1539, the imperial aspect of the assembly is introduced:

> God standeth in the congregacyon of prynces: he
> Is Iudge amonge Goddes.

The Geneva Bible of 1560 follows the Vulgate:

> God standeth in the assemblie of gods: he
> iudgeth among gods.

The Bishops' Bible of 1568 modifies this but little:

> God standeth in the congregation of God: he
> iudgeth in the midst of God.

---

[1] *Tetrachordon:* "They of best note who have translated the scripture since, and Diodati for one, ..."

The Authorized Version apparently sought a compromise:

> God standeth in the congregation of the mighty;
> he judgeth among the gods.

George Buchanan's Latin metrical version of the Psalms has gone much farther in emphasizing the imperial aspect of the assembly than any of the texts:

> Regum timendorum, in proprios greges,
> Reges in ipsos imperium est Jovae,
> Qui judicantum examinabit
> Nequitiam trutina severa.

But it remained for the standard psalter of Milton's youth, that of Sternhold and Hopkins, to dispense entirely with the divine aspect of the assembly:

> Amid the prease with men of might,
> the Lord himselfe doth stand:
> To plead the cause of truth and right,
> with Judges of the land.

Which one of these various readings influenced Milton most in the final expression of his translation it would be almost impossible to determine. The metrical version of Buchanan and that of Sternhold and Hopkins would both have been of considerable importance to his own version, if for no other reason than that their metrical form was the same as the one he was using. Added to that is the significant fact that he was perfectly familiar with both of them—as was every churchgoer, for that matter. In both of these earlier versions the line "Of kings and lordly states" is more than merely suggested; it is part of each of them.

From the same general sources, and they are in both cases *only* general, came the double verb of the last line of Milton's first stanza. His two verbs, "judges" and "debates," while apparently derived from the one word, יִשְׁפֹּט, are in reality derived from the second and the first verb, נְצָב, in the Hebrew. The first verb, נְצָב, a niphal of נָצַב, conveys the idea in that stem of "taking one's stand," so that the figure becomes that of a presiding judge in a law court, hearing and judging cases, partaking of the same meaning as in Exod. 7:15 and again in 34:2. The second verb, יִשְׁפֹּט, Milton has made yield him two, a device of which he is fond, but he specifically warns of the original by giving a transliteration of the Hebrew word in the margin. In this instance, the "debates" is a carry-over from נְצָב, and as such it advances and adds to the richness of the translation, rather than producing any positive gain in so far as the verse is concerned, even though it is there apparently for rhyme purposes.

In the same way the italicized line is an outgrowth from the Hebrew, the two different lines of translations proceeding from the Hebrew word אֵל. This word was taken by some translators to mean only "God," or Deity in some aspect, from the first syllable of אֱלֹהִים. But the word in Hebrew is often employed without divine significance, as in Ps. 18:3 and Exod. 15:11, or as in Ezra 31:11, אֵל גּוֹיִם, spoken of Nebuchadnezzar. Milton has again translated it in the same general manner as in this verse in Ps. 80:11, where אַרְזֵי־אֵל, means literally "cedars of God," which is really an idiomatic expression meaning "the loftiest or highest of their kind,"[1] by the phrase "cedars tall."

The same duality of idea which operated upon a word was again employed to extract from בְּקֶרֶב the

[1] Cf. Baldwin, *op. cit.*, p. 458.

needed amount of material for the completion of the
third line. The word בְּקֶרֶב means "in-midst-of," and is
translated "among" in the first line and used again in the
third line as "on both his hands," so that the fullest meaning of the Hebrew is brought out and metrical purposes
served by the same operation.

In the second verse the original is so plainly simple
that but little change may be noted in the various
translations. The Hebrew with translation reads:

עַד־מָתַי תִּשְׁפְּטוּ־עָוֶל וּפְנֵי רְשָׁעִים תִּשְׂאוּ־סֶלָה , "How long
will ye judge perversely and faces of wicked regard?"

The Vulgate and Tremellius, respectively:

> Usque iudicatis iniquitatem: et facies
> peccatorum sumitis?

> Quousque judicabitis inique et personam
> improboram suscipietis summe.

The various other textual versions differ from these two
but little; however, the Sternhold and Hopkins metrical
rendering is of interest:

> How long, said he will you proceed,
>   false judgment to award:
> And have respect for love of meed,
>   the wicked to regard?

In this verse the Hebrew employs the verb שָׁפַט ,
meaning "to judge," with the adverbial modifier, עָוֶל ,
meaning "perversely" (a noun used as an adjective,
from the root עָוַל , meaning "to be wrong" or "*perverse*").
Milton has altered this arrangement somewhat by using
"pervert" as a verb and substantivizing the "judging"
idea, but still retaining the original modification by employing the two adjectives "false" and "wrong" in con-

nection with "judgment." This constitutes a treatment of the original in such a way as to produce at once fuller expression of the content and a larger amount of metrical material with which to work. Had he remained as terse as his original, his second verse would have read

> How long will ye pervert the right
> . . . .
> Favoring the wicked?

The result secured by the addition of an extra line to translate the first clause of the original, and then of a line and a half in italics to fill out the quatrain, may not have produced good poetry, but it fulfilled the metrical requirement without violating the Hebrew meaning.

In the third verse, none of the textual or metrical English versions employ the meaning of the first verb of the Hebrew in their translations. The Hebrew reads: שִׁפְטוּ־דָל וְיָתוֹם עָנִי וָרָשׁ הַצְדִּיקוּ, "Judge ye poor and fatherless pronounce innocent desolate and needy."

All of the Latin versions or paraphrases retained the verb "to judge," but of the English, the Coverdale, the Great, the Geneva, and the Authorized versions employ some other verb, the Geneva using "do right to," the Bishops' using "judge," and the others employing "defend," as did Sternhold and Hopkins, whose arrangement follows:

> Whereas of due you should defend
> the fatherlesse and weake:
> And when the poore man doth contend,
> in iudgment iustly speak.

None of these were exactly models for Milton's version, although there are some points of similarity between some of them and his. He wrote thus:

> Regard the weak and fatherless;
> Despatch the poor man's cause;
> And raise the man in deep distress
> By just and equal laws.

This is more properly an expansion of the Hebrew than any interpolation of another translation. Milton evidently felt, as the absence of italics indicates, that he was not sufficiently changing the meaning of the original to call for any explanation whatever.

The succeeding verses offer but little source for comment, as but one phrase appears in italics, and this is obviously a metrical and rhyme concession.

In the seventh verse, however, there is an apparent discrepancy between Milton's version and the original which calls for explanation. The Hebrew reads:

אָכֵן כְּאָדָם תְּמוּתוּן וּכְאַחַד הַשָּׂרִים תִּפֹּלוּ, "But like man ye shall die and like one of the princes ye shall fall."

Milton has made this:

> But ye shall die like men, and fall
> as other princes *die.*

Here he apparently mistook the word אֶחָד, "one," for the closely similar word אַחֵר, "other."[1] Such an explanation, however, will not suffice, for there are too many other translations which have made the same mistake, if that was what it originally was. True, the Vulgate has rightly translated the Hebrew:

> Vos autem sicut homines moriemini: et sicut
> unus de principibus cadetis.

The Targum and the Syriac follow the Hebrew here very closely, but other translations do not. Tremellius included both words "one" and "other" in his Latin:

[1] Cf. Baldwin, *op. cit.*, p. 461.

> At certe un plebeius homo morituri estis,
> sicut unus aliorum principum casuri estis.

Diodati did practically the same thing in Italian:

> Tuttavolta voi morrete come un'altro uomo,
> e caerete come qualunque *altro* de'principi.

Of the English textual versions, Coverdale has "& fall like one of the tyrauntes." The Great Bible has "and fall lyke one of the princes." But the Geneva of 1560 reads "& ye princes, shall fall like others." This reading is retained and modified in the Bishops' Bible, "and princes them selues shall fall away lyke as other [do]." The Sternhold and Hopkins metrical version has so far departed from the original substance of the Hebrew in the effort to secure four lines for the Hebraic two that the resulting form is of little direct significance here:

> But notwithstanding you shall die
> as men and so decay:
> O tyrants I shall you destroy
> and plucke you quite away.

It is evident from an examination of these various versions that something other than a misunderstanding of the Hebrew original was operating on Milton's rendering here, for too many forms of the original were accessible to him to suppose that he was not as well aware of the possibilities of this verse as anyone reasonably could be. The change from the one form to the other involved so slight a change that to point out the same procedure in other versions is enough to settle the matter.

Psalm 82, just analyzed, is sufficiently typical of the other eight translated to make such minute analysis of them unnecessary. The remaining Psalms raise the same kinds of problems in precisely the same ways, and the foregoing analysis of the one will serve as a basis for several important conclusions regarding the entire translation project.

A. THE NATURE OF THE VERSE FORM

It is probable, as Masson pointed out,[1] that in these Psalm translations of 1648 Milton was led to make his experiment by the interest which was then felt both in England and in Scotland in the project, which was several years old, of a complete new version of the Psalms, which would supersede, in public worship, the old English version of Sternhold and Hopkins first published in 1562, and likewise the version, partly the same, that had been in use in Scotland since 1565, known as Lekprevik's, from the name of the printer who had first published it in Edinburgh. In spite of competing versions these two had remained substantially the authorized psalters in the two countries till the meeting of the Long Parliament. After the meeting of that body, and especially after the Westminster Assembly had been convoked to aid it in religious matters in July, 1643, a revision or renovation of the psalter had been discussed. This became one of the matters which the Westminster Assembly was especially required to deliberate and report to the Parliament. Consequently there had been considerable activity already made in urging the claims of various versions, in print or in manuscript, by persons recently dead or still living. Among such versions there was one by the distinguished and pious Francis Rous, member of the Long Parliament and also a lay member of the Westminster Assembly.

[1] David Masson, *The Poetical Works*, I (London, 1896), 77.

This version was first printed in 1641, had gained many friends, and in 1645 a carefully revised edition of it was recommended by the Assembly to Parliament. The House of Commons was well satisfied with this version, written, as it was, by a Commoner, but the Lords had previously taken up a rival version by William Barton of Oxford, first published in 1644, and were slow to turn to Rous. The matter became deadlocked, and was never settled so far as England was concerned.

Milton evidently had some aspect of the controversy in mind when he chose the form of his verse, for he adopted the ordinary service meter of eights and sixes, rhyming the first and third lines as well as the second and fourth.

This form is important in this discussion for two reasons: the metrical pattern adopted was certain to leave its mark upon the material, and the versions already existent in this form were equally certain to wield a direct control over the translation.

So far as Milton's translation of the Hebrew is concerned, there is, on the basis of the Psalm just analyzed, no warrant for assuming in a single instance that his difficulty lay in the understanding of the Hebrew. I have not found a single deviation, in the whole nine Psalms, which on close examination would indicate a deviation from the original Hebrew because of any misunderstanding of the text. But when possible influences on Milton's translation are considered as coming from the number and nature of the Psalm versions which he knew—and the number with which we can connect him is by no means all of the versions he may have known—the importance of these other versions for him becomes very remarkable.

Had he chosen to employ any other than the hymn form, it would be more difficult, but not impossible, to discover the effect on him of whatever versions existed in the form he had selected. But when he selected, as he did select, the very form which was employed by the hymnal prosodists of the sixteenth century and of his own day, and when it is possible to point out, as I have just done, the large number of correspondences between Milton's expressions and the expressions of others essaying the same task, the inference is clear that all such metrical translations or adaptations had their several effects upon his translation, as did every other version which he knew. Evidently it was not the translation of the Hebrew which bothered him.

The Psalm translations, therefore, yield quite definite indications that Milton read their Hebrew original with ease and facility; but his metrical arrangement of them remains the poorest of all his poetry, for the difficulty was more than ability to translate Hebrew, which anyone may learn in time to do; it was rather that Milton failed dismally to make effective employment of the hymn form. He who wrote some of the most pleasing lyrics in the English language could not, because of his nature, fitly employ one of the lowliest poetic forms English genius has produced.

II. PARADISE LOST

A. THE RELATION OF THE SEMITIC MATERIAL EMPLOYED
TO THE TREATMENT OF THE THEME

Because of the nature of the material employed, because of the skeletal projection of the work, and because
of the employment of many unavoidable details, *Paradise
Lost* possesses a peculiar relationship to the Semitic
material and influence which lay back of these three
aspects, and just what this relationship is, and, more
specifically, why it is, becomes a question to be answered
at this point.

Throughout the major portion of *Paradise Lost*, if not
throughout all of it, the material employed is, of course,
readily recognized as having been primarily of Semitic
origin. The story of the fall of man, the story of the fall
of the angels, the conception of Satan, the story of creation, the entire Eden myth—all are of undeniably
Semitic origin, and for Milton the prime source for the
entire poem was, by the very nature of the material, the
Old Testament. The entire underlying groundwork of the
poem was, obviously, Semitic; and apparently Milton's
debt to Semitic sources is very large indeed. But just as
such a concession is about to be granted, other facts force
themselves into consideration in such a manner as to reset
the entire problem of source in its proper light.

Paradise Lost, in theme and in treatment, and
Goethe's *Faust* are similar in that both poems, for such
they both are, were no more than supreme treatments of
what had come to be perfectly conventionalized subjects

with ages of development back of them which had crystallized both in form and material to such an extent that in both works the ultimate outcome, given the supreme artist, was almost predictable, and certainly was already set before either writer put pen to paper. The genius of both Milton and Goethe consists, not in the creation of their material, but in the ordering and marshaling of its parts, and, to a certain extent, in the lack of such ordering and marshaling, for each work depends a good deal for its greatness upon its ultimate chaotic nature, the chaotic nature of the supremely great.

So conventionalized had Milton's material for *Paradise Lost* become by his time that the larger indebtedness to Semitic sources fails entirely to function, for his material came to him, not from Hebraic or other Semitic books or manuscript, but from insular and continental vernacular literature, the literature of the various vulgar European languages. Almost every European tongue had its own form and version for the major incidents of the theme; nearly all had the entire theme worked out in more or less detail. It is not at all remarkable that *Paradise Lost* was antedated by Andreini's *Adamo* in Italy (1613), by Grotius' *Adamus Exul* in Holland (1601), by Vondel's *Lucifer* (1654), in the same country, and by Du Bartas' *Divine Weeks and Works* in France (English translation in 1605). To misunderstand the relationship of these works and scores of others like them is to misunderstand the whole nature of Milton's epic, for the fact is that he purposely set out to recast the bits of material which he had collected over a period of at least twenty years[1] in such a way as to "justify the ways of God to man,"

---

[1] Cf. Masson, *Poetical Works*, II (London, 1896), 16 ff.

and he selected for the setting of his immense theme the largest dimensional scope which he or his age could supply —the setting of the whole scheme of man's relationship to the universe and to Deity. The material for this setting he found ready at hand in the age-old story of creation and the fall of man, which provided him at once with characters and stage of such a scope as was commensurable with his theme.

Nearly every phase of setting, stage, and characters, all originally Semitic it is true, had, long before Milton's time, become overlarded and overlaid with strata which represented the accumulated deposits of preceding ages, eras, civilizations, so that the originally Semitic material and treatment were no longer directly Semitic at all, but rather what this originally Semitic treatment and material had become in passing through the various and sundry languages and literatures into which they had passed and been absorbed. This transmutation does not affect the biblical tinge which so plainly tinctures Milton's conceptions of his material in this poem, for, as has been pointed out in connection with the discussion of the Psalms in an earlier chapter, in spite of his protestations to the contrary, the Bible and all that was biblical implied for him and his age the whole adumbrated mass of commentary, redaction, and exegesis, whether Jewish or gentile, which had become directly attached to the text of Scripture.

Those larger details of the skeletal outline of the poem, viz., the creation material, the fall of the angels, the Eden story, and the fall of man, are not, therefore, to be conceived of as having been primarily and directly of Semitic origin in any of the literary treatments of them throughout the Renaissance or the sixteenth and seventeenth centuries. In their general outlines and plans these treatments had, from Dante's conception of the *Inferno* down to Andreini's *Adamo*, become occidentalized to a European generality of conception which prevented any direct Semitic influence altering or affecting their larger outlines, which had become permanently fixed by the operation upon them of poetry, drama, and mime through and following the Middle Ages. Not in the larger conceptions of *Paradise Lost* may genuinely direct Semitic traces be found; the possibility of such traces existing in them is closed.

Where, then, may specific Semitic influences be found in *Paradise Lost*, if not in what at first appear to be the most Semitic of all the elements of the poem? The answer to this question is that direct Semitic influences in *Paradise Lost* operate in a peculiar way, and the amount, the significance, and the result of such influences are large, taken either separately or in aggregate, because of the manner in which they operate.

The chief elements which make up the material of *Paradise Lost* are, as has been stated, remarkable for the manner in which they have been treated. This treatment is one of the great secrets, if not the greatest secret, of Milton's genius; just how he secured the results he did secure does not and will not appear, although, as Samuel Johnson observed in the biography, they are "variously conjectured by men who cannot bear to think themselves ignorant of that which, at last, neither diligence nor sagacity can discover." Waiving Johnson's problem, it is possible to discover that the larger aspects of the poem owe their majestic result to the marvelous certainty of Milton's employment of detail. In the details of the larger conceptions of the setting and movement of the poem, in those wonderful minutiae which the high art of the poet wove into continually larger patterns, is packed all of the lore, all of the learning, all of the remembered experiences of his teeming mind that find their way into the epic. And here it is, in these detailed embellishments, in these filigree works which ultimately constitute and support the beautiful grandeur of the poem, here it is that Semitic influence appears, in many instances brazenly, as if to ask, "What are you going to do about my being here?"; in others, subdued, almost submerged, so as to be unnoticed by casual investigation. Exactly how much of such material there is, I do not know; some of it I have in a measure charted and explored; more that I am aware of I find escaping me for a time, for whosoever follows the subtle ramifications of Milton's mental imagery treads a brilliantly lighted path, but a long one.

B. THE MUSE OF MILTON'S SONG

The figure whom Milton was invoking in the opening of the first Book of *Paradise Lost* is an elusive one, as Verity's partial summary of what has been said of her would indicate.[1] In the invocation of the opening lines Milton says:

> Sing, Heavenly Muse, that on the secret top
> Of Oreb, or of Sinai, didst inspire
> That shepherd who first taught the chosen seed
> In the beginning how the Heavens and Earth
> Rose out of Chaos. Or, if Sion hill
> Delight thee more, and Siloa's brook that flowed
> Fast by the oracle of God, I thence

[1] A. W. Verity, *Paradise Lost* (Cambridge, 1910), pp. 686–88.

> Invoke thy aid to my adventurous song,
> That with no middle flight intends to soar
>
> . . . .
>
> And chiefly thou, O Spirit, that dost prefer
> Before all temples the upright heart and pure,
> Instruct me, for thou know'st; thou from the first,
> Wast present, and, with mighty wings outspread,
> Dove-like sat'st brooding
>
> . . . .
>
> Say first (for Heaven hides nothing from thy view,
> Nor the deep tract of Hell)

At the beginning of Book VII, halfway through the poem, Milton again turned to his muse, as if pausing at the middle ground of his endeavor for a fresh start. In this second invocational address there appears the name Urania and certain other peculiarities, which, in so far as the other and earlier figure addressed is concerned, result in a "distinction without a difference":

> Descend from Heaven, Urania, by that name
> If rightly thou art called, whose voice divine
> Following, above the Olympian hill I soar,
>
> . . . .
>
> The meaning, not the name, I call; for thou
> Nor of the Muses nine, nor on the top
> Of old Olympus dwell'st; but Heavenly-born,
> Before the hills appeared or fountain flowed,
> Thou with eternal Wisdom didst converse,
> Wisdom thy sister, and with her didst play
> In presence of the Almighty Father, pleased
> With thy celestial song.
>
> . . . .
>
> In darkness, and with dangers compassed round,
> And solitude; yet not alone, while thou
> Visit'st my slumbers nightly, or when morn

> Purples the east. Still govern thou my song,
> Urania, and fit audience find though few;
> . . . .
> So fail not thou who thee implores;
> For thou art Heavenly.[1]

Once more the figure is invoked in *Paradise Regained*, this time as in the opening of *Paradise Lost*, without a name:

> Thou Spirit, who led'st this glorious Eremite
> Into the desert, his victorious field
> Against the spiritual foe, and brought'st him thence
> By proof of the undoubted Son of God, inspire,
> As thou art wont, my prompted song, else mute. . . . .[2]

It is quite evident in all three of these invocations that the name of the Spirit addressed, contrary to Dunster,[3] is of little moment; and that in Book I and Book VII of *Paradise Lost* there is some common basis in the two invocational addresses which lies in the Spirit addressed, for the statement: "Thou from the first wast present . . . ."[4] is too nearly like "Before the hills appeared or fountain flowed, Thou. . . . ."[5] Also, from insistence upon the biblical character of the Spirit in the two invocations in *Paradise Lost*, they tend to unite with one another, while from the expression in *Paradise Regained*, "Inspire as thou art wont, my prompted song, else mute, ..."[6] it is evident that Milton was addressing the muse which he had invoked before.

[1] *Paradise Lost*, Bk. VII, ll. 1–12, 27–31, 38–39.

[2] *Paradise Regained*, Bk. I, ll. 8–12.

[3] C. Dunster, *Considerations on Milton's Early Reading and the Prima Stamina of Paradise Lost* (London, 1800).

[4] *Paradise Lost*, Bk. I, ll. 19–20.

[5] *Op. cit.*, Bk. VII, l. 8.

[6] *Paradise Regained*, Bk. I, ll. 11–12.

It has been variously assumed that in *Paradise Lost*,
Book I, two muses were being addressed; that lines 1–17
refer to one muse, and lines 17–26 to another. Such an
apparent duality of muses appears again in the opening
panegyric of Book III of *Paradise Lost*, where it is very
striking. Verity, who prepared a special section of his
prodigious notes for this particular point,[1] has quite clearly pointed out the different muses whom Milton addressed, without explaining, however, why Milton should
have been as polygamous in his employment of poetical
muses as he was in theoretical speculation in the *De
doctrina Christiana*. Were there any purpose served by
the plurality of muses involved, were any greater insight
into an understanding of the poet's intention in the
invocations forthcoming from conceiving of more than
one, possibly of more than two, muses, certainly the case
for such plurality would be possessed of ample support.
But such is not the case.

In accepting more than one muse there is a resulting
obscurity of the invocational passages which only increases with the addition of the passage at the beginning of
Book III of *Paradise Lost*:

> Hail, holy Light, offspring of Heaven first-born!
> Or of the Eternal coeternal beam
> May I express thee unblamed? since God is light,
> And never but in unapproached light
> Dwelt from eternity, dwelt then in thee,
> Bright effluence of bright essence increate!
> . . . .
>
>   Before the sun,
> Before the Heavens, thou wert, and at the voice
> Of God, as with a mantle, didst invest

[1] Verity, *op. cit.*, pp. 686 ff.

> The rising World of waters dark and deep,
> Won from the void and formless infinite!
> Thee I revisit now with bolder wing,
> Escaped the Stygian pool, though long detained
> In that obscure sojourn, while in my flight,
> . . . .
> Taught by the Heavenly Muse to venture down
> The dark descent, and up to re-ascend,
> Though hard and rare: thee I revisit safe,
> And feel thy sovran vital lamp; but thou
> Revisit'st not these eyes,
> . . . .
> So much the rather thou, celestial Light,
> Shine inward, and the mind through all her powers
> Irradiate: there plant eyes, all mist from thence
> Purge and disperse, that I may see and tell
> Of things invisible to mortal sight.[1]

Here is apparently a third muse to add to the two pointed out in Book I by Verity, who states that the "Spirit" of line 17 is expressly distinguished from the Holy Spirit, who is invoked in the earlier lines, again in line 19 of Book III, and in *Paradise Regained*. But something more than this is necessary in order to secure the wealth of material which Milton put into these invocations, and the fulness of them he himself explained in the chapter, "Of the Holy Spirit," in *De doctrina Christiana*. He there speaks at length of the Holy Spirit, describing its nature:

With regard to the nature of the Spirit, in what manner it exists, or whence it arose, Scripture is silent; which is a caution to us not to be too hasty in our conclusions on the subject. For though it be a Spirit . . . . yet in treating of the nature of the Holy Spirit, we are not authorized to infer from such expressions, that the Spirit was bequeathed from the Father and the Son. . . . . The

[1] *Paradise Lost*, Bk. III, ll. 1–6, 8–15, 19–23, 51–55.

Spirit is neither said to be generated nor created, nor is any other mode of existence specifically attributed to it in Scriptures. . . . .

The name of the Spirit is frequently applied to God and angels, and to the human mind. . . . . Sometimes it means Christ, who, according to the common opinion, was sent by the Father to lead the Israelites into the land of Canaan. . . . . Sometimes it means that impulse or voice of God by which the prophets were inspired. . . . . Sometimes it means that light of truth, whether ordinary or extraordinary, wherewith God enlightens and leads his people. . . . . More particularly, it implies that light which was shed on Christ himself. . . . . It is also used to signify the spiritual gifts conferred by God on individuals, and the art of the gift itself. . . . .

Nothing can be more certain, than that all these passages . . . . [the biblical references omitted here by means of which Milton supported every one of these statements] and many others of a similar kind, in the Old Testament, were understood of the virtue and power of the Father. . . . . So likewise under the Gospel, what is called the Holy Spirit, or the Spirit of God, sometimes means the Father himself. . . . .

Again, it sometimes means the virtue and power of the Father. . . . .

Thirdly, the Spirit signifies a devine impulse, or light, or voice, or word, transmitted from above, either through Christ, who is the word of God, or by some other channel. . . . . Lastly, the Spirit signifies the person itself of the Holy Spirit, or its symbol. . . . .

Lastly, it signifies the donation of the Spirit itself, and of its attendant gifts.

From such a discussion, it is fairly obvious that the Spirit invoked in *Paradise Regained* to lead Christ into the battleground of the Wilderness is the same as that aspect of the Holy Spirit who "according to the common opinion, was sent by the Father to lead the Israelites into the land of Canaan."

The Spirit addressed in the opening lines of Book III of *Paradise Lost* identifies itself with that "light of truth,

whether ordinary or extraordinary, wherewith God enlightens and leads his people," and "that light which was
shed on Christ himself." In so far as the Heavenly Muse
is concerned, it will be noted that Milton has said in the
De doctrina that the Holy Spirit "is also used to signify
the spiritual gifts conferred by God on individuals, and
the act of gift itself."

Clearly Milton conceived of his muse, not as a
plurality, not as now one, now another, muse, but as one
Muse, appearing and appealing under different aspects.

Saurat[1] has noted the absence of dogma in Milton,
concluding that he looked upon dogma as a sort of myth,
chiefly useful for poetical purposes. Certainly it appears,
in his conception of the Holy Spirit in *Paradise Lost* and
Paradise Regained, that he was employing a myth so
tenuous that he might, without such indications as he
uses in the *De doctrina*, shift from one phase to another of
the same Spirit without in any way warning his reader.
But the treatment of the Holy Spirit in the *De doctrina
Christiana* fully explains the various invocations of the
poems, and it becomes evident that the Spirit invoked—
and there was but one such Spirit—was conceived of
under various aspects, each of which is recognizable when
present in the poems only by means of the clarity of the
aspects of such a Spirit set forth in the *De doctrina
Christiana*.

There remains the question of where such a conception
of the Holy Spirit as Milton has presented came from:
Where did he find the ingredients from which he built the
elaborate structure which appears in the *De doctrina?* He
says there that there is no specific information on the

---

[1] Denis Saurat, *Milton: Man and Thinker* (New York, 1925), p. 203.

subject in the Old Testament, and so far as the rise and
origin of the Holy Spirit, there is nothing in the New
Testament that bears on the subject. Where, then, did
his conception come from?

The nearest approach of any such multiple-natured
conception of a Holy Spirit to Milton's is in the Jewish
Shekinah, which arose as a conception in the rabbinical
comment and saying attached to the Hebrew Scripture.

The Shekinah (שכינה), literally, "the dwelling,"
was the majestic presence or manifestation of God which
had descended to "dwell" in this mundane sphere, sent
forth by God, or come from him, to "dwell" among men.
Like *Memra* ("word," or "logos") and *Yekara* (*kabod*, or
"glory"), the term "Shekinah" was used by the rabbis in
place of God when the anthropomorphic expressions of
the biblical text were no longer regarded as proper. The
word itself, around which developed almost a literature,
was taken from such passages as speak of God as "dwelling" either in the Tabernacle or among the people of
Israel.[1] Occasionally the name of God is spoken of as
descending.[2] It is especially said that God dwells in
Jerusalem,[3] on Mount Zion,[4] and in the Temple itself.[5]
Allusion is also made to "him that dwelt in the bush,"[6]
and it is said that "the glory of the Lord abode upon
Mount Sinai."[7] The term "Shekinah," which is Hebrew,
whereas *Memra* and *Yekara* are Aramaic, took the place

[1] Exod. 25:8, 19; 45:6; Num. 5:3; 35:34; I Kings 6:13; Ezek. 43:9;
Zech. 2:14 (A.V., 10).

[2] Deut. 12:11; 14:23; 16:6; 11; 26:2; Neh. 1:9.

[3] Zech. 8:3; Ps. 134:21; I Chron. 23:25.

[4] Isa. 8:18; Joel 4 (A.V., 3):17, 21; Pss. 15:1; 74:2.

[5] Ezek. 43:7.   [6] Deut. 33:16.   [7] Exod. 24:16.

of the latter two in Talmud and Midrasch, and thus absorbed the meaning which they have in the Targum, where they almost exclusively occur. However, the word "Shekinah" occurs most frequently in the Aramaic versions, since they were intended for the people and were even read to them, and since precautions had therefore to be taken against possible misunderstandings in regard to the conception of God. The word "dwell" in the Hebrew text is accordingly rendered in the Targumim by the phrase "Let the Shekinah rest."[1] Onkelos translated *Elohim* (אֱלֹהִים), in Genesis 9:27, by Shekinah; and wherever the person, the dwelling, or the remoteness of God is mentioned, he paraphrased by the same word;[2] so too, wherever the Tetragrammaton occurs, he substituted for it the term "Shekinah,"[3] and "presence" or "face" was translated the same way.[4] Targumim pseudo-Jonathan and Yerushalmi adopt a like system.[5] When the text states that God dwells in the Temple above the Cherubim,[6] or that God has been seen,[7] the Yerushalmi has Shekinah; and even where it describes God as abiding in heaven, the same word is used.[8] The Temple is called

---

[1] Exod. 25:8, 19, 45–46; Num. 5:3; 35:34; Deut. 32:10 (R.V.: "He compassed him about"); Ps. 74:2.

[2] Num. 14:14, 42; 16:3; 35:34; Deut. 1:42; 3:24; 4:39; 6:15; 7:21; 23:16; 31:17.

[3] Deut. 12:5, 11, 21.

[4] Exod. 33:14–15; Num. 6:25; Deut. 31:17–18.

[5] Pss. 16:8; 89:47; Lam. 2:19; Cant. 6:1.

[6] Hab. 2:20; I Sam. 4:4; II Sam. 6:2; I Kings 8:12, 13; 14:21; Ps. 74:2.

[7] Isa. 6:6; Exod. 3:6; Ezek. 1:1; Lev. 9:4.

[8] Isa. 33:5; Deut. 3:24; 4:39.

the "house of the Shekinah,"[1] and the term likewise occurs in connection with glory[2] and with "holiness."[3]

In the New Testament, the sole Greek equivalent for the word "Shekinah" is δόξα,[4] which occurs in those passages which mention "radiance" in New Testament or apocryphal writings; although the Shekinah is perhaps implied in John 1:14 and Rev. 21:3, where the words σκηνουν and σκηνή are used respectively. The idea that God dwells in man and that man is his temple[5] is merely a more realistic conception of the resting of the Shekinah on man.

The Muse of *Paradise Lost* and *Paradise Regained*, which was found to be not only single, but a poetic usage of the Holy Spirit set forth in the *De doctrina Christiana*, ultimately, therefore, goes back to a Semitic origin, which is much more apparent in the poetic than in the prose treatment of it.

Milton's conception of the Holy Spirit was derived from his reading of Targums and Talmud, for, as he himself said, the Scripture alone did not directly supply such a conception as that at which he arrived. To his rabbinical reading must be allotted this conception of the Holy Spirit, and the effect of the rabbinical origin is very apparent wherever in *Paradise Lost* the Muse appears. She is employed vicariously for various acts, manifestations, and attributes of the Almighty, appearing as the

[1] Targ. Onk. to Deut. 12:5; Pss. 49:15; 108:8.

[2] *Yekara,* Ruth 2:12; Cant. 3:6; 4:6; 5:6; Pss. 44:25; 68:19; 115:16; Jer. 19:18.

[3] Cant. 1:10; 2:2; 3:2; 6:1; Pss. 74:12; 86:3.

[4] Col. 2:9; II Cor. 6:16; John 14:23.

[5] Joseph Meade, *Works* (London, 1674), p. 343.

Spirit (רוּחַ) which was brooding over (מְרַחֶפֶת), the waters of the original Chaos in the act of Creation, and later in the poem is represented as having been sent out with the Son in order that the two might generate from Chaos the Visible Universe. She again appears as Light, that, for Milton, most potent of all divine attributes, which in Book III receives the greatest homage which the poet anywhere, in any of his work, bestowed on any person or conception, human or divine, not all of which was due to the fact that he was physically blind.

The connection between the Muse of Milton's song and the Semitic Shekinah is subtle, well hidden in unknown or forgotten affiliations of English or European thought and language with oriental lore, but, on the other hand, in linking the Muse of the poems or the Holy Spirit of the theological system with the Semitic שכינה , the former is clarified completely, and the latter is greatly illuminated.

C. THE RABBINICAL EMBELLISHMENTS OF THE STORY OF THE FALL OF MAN

The story of the fall of man, as set forth in all its wealth of detail in *Paradise Lost*, contains in those very details an immense amount of rabbinical lore, so much so, in fact, that the entire story is embellished by one rabbinical or Semitic element after another, which embellishment was effected with the utmost adroitness on the part of Milton. This adroitness of application consisted in employing these elements in the very heart of the poem, Book IX, and part of Book X. These books contain the actual climactic movement of the plot of the poem, which is the dramatic episode of the fall of man, prepared for, and introduced by, the first eight books, having provided a setting of the proper scope for the climax.

When Milton had, by means of the proper amount of discussion of the fallen angels, led, by means of dialogue, through the great panorama of creation, the warfare in heaven, the resultant fall of the angels, and the creation of man, he had finally, but not until then, set his stage for the climax of the poem, which was the fall of man, or the losing of paradise. His problem, once his stage was set, was to introduce Satan to the Garden of Eden and then to bring him into direct contact with Adam and Eve in order that there might be so effected that design with which Satan originally left the Infernal Conclave.

Satan was therefore made to approach the Garden, and then, having entered, he

> on the Tree of Life
> Sat like a cormorant [1]

surveying the place. This figure of the cormorant is the first of many disguises adopted by Satan during his sojourn in Eden and requires an explanation.

Rabbinical tradition in Midrasch and Masorah had very early considered the question of how Satan appeared to Eve, and what Eve took him to be when he finally did appear to her.

As early as the twelfth-century Book of Adam,[2] Satan, or Iblis, is made to attempt to make use of a bird, the peacock, to effect his approach to, and connection with, the human pair; but failed to induce the peacock to grant his request. However, when the peacock refused to

---

[1] *Paradise Lost*, Bk. IV, ll. 194, 196.

[2] Migne, *Enc. Theol.*, 24:39 ff.; also G. Weil, *Biblische Legenden der Muselmänner* (1845).

accede to his wishes, she agreed to bring to him for his
purposes the serpent. The serpent in the Book of Adam
is of a vaguely suggested form, but is some kind of quadruped resembling now a camel and now some indetermin-
ate animal. Iblis prevails upon the serpent to conduct him
into the Garden and thence to Eve, and enters the mouth
of the serpent and speaks to Eve from his lurking-place
among the teeth of the serpent.

In the Midrasch Hag-gadol (מדרש הגדל)[1] Satan
(Sameel, סמאל) is made to consider the resplendent
serpent shaped like a גמל (camel) as an instrument of
his approach to man. Like the strange quadruped of the
Book of Adam, the precise form of the גמל is uncertain,
except that it was the form of an animal.

Such rabbinical material as this underwent considerable amplification and change during the Middle Ages,
and by Milton's time had taken on generalizations and
significances which had become a distinct part of the
temptation material. Joseph Meade summarized the
whole of the rabbinical tradition for seventeenth-century
England as follows:

Spirits, good or bad, might appear to man, as the Old Testament plentifully records, at almost any time and under almost any
conditions, but before the Fall, evil Spirits or Satan might not
appear in human shape, for man as yet preserved his integrity, and
therefore Satan, because he was a Spirit fallen from his first glorious
perfection, might only appear in some shape as might argue his
imperfection and abasement, which was in the shape of a being
inferior to man.[2]

Several aspects of this tradition have been employed
in *Paradise Lost* in order to bring Satan into contact with

[1] S. Schechter, מדרש הגדל (Cambridge, 1902), pp. 86 ff.

[2] Meade, *Works*, p. 224.

the human pair which was his goal. He first appeared as a cormorant, who saw all of the Garden, including Adam and Eve, without, however, their seeing him. His next move after his preliminary survey was to get nearer to his prime object, man, to accomplish which he alighted from his lofty stand and mingled with

> the sportful herd
> Of those four-footed kinds, himself now one.[1]

Apparently he then assumed various shapes for his reconnoitering:

> A lion now he stalks with fiery glare;
> Then as a tiger, who by chance hath spied
> In some purlieu two gentle fawns at play,
> Straight couches close; then, rising, changes oft
> His couchant watch, as one who chose his ground,
> Whence rushing he might surest seize them both,
> Griped in each paw.[2]

In one of these animal shapes he approached near enough to be able to overhear the conversation of the human pair as they addressed each other, and the implication seems to be at this point that Adam and Eve were for the first time observing Satan without being precisely aware of him apart from the other animals who were disporting themselves about them, as in Book IX Eve pays little or no attention to the serpent when he first begins his gyrations:

> So varied he, and of his tortuous train
> Curled many a wanton wreath in sight of Eve,
> To lure her eye; she, busied, heard the sound
> Of rustling leaves, but minded not, as used
> To such disport before her through the field,
> From every beast.[3]

[1] *Paradise Lost*, Bk. IV, ll. 396–97.
[2] *Op. cit.*, Bk. IV, ll. 402–8.
[3] *Op. cit.*, Bk. IX, ll. 516–21.

While Satan was thus eavesdropping, Adam entered upon a most remarkable statement to Eve, to which Satan listened most attentively, for Adam was informing Eve of the mandate laid against the eating of the fruit of the Tree of the Knowledge of Good and Evil.

In this device which Milton employed for conveying the information regarding the mandate against the Tree of Knowledge to Satan, he was following very strictly in the path of rabbinical tradition. Rabbinical comment upon Scripture and outgrowths from that comment had long dwelt upon the question of how Satan knew, as he appeared to know in his subsequent conversation with Eve, all about the Tree and the mandate laid against it. The generality of rabbinical opinion, in the Book of the Bee[1] and elsewhere, settled upon Satan's having learned of the interdict by overhearing Adam impart the information to Eve. The Book of the Bee contains a thirteenth-century form of the tradition, as follows:

After Eve was created, Adam told her the story of the tree [of good and evil], and Satan overheard it, and by his envy it became the occasion and cause of their being made to sin, and being expelled from Paradise.[2]

How closely Milton followed his Semitic model here is apparent in Satan's soliloquy which follows Adam's statement to Eve, for Satan says therein:

> let me not forget what I have
> gained
> From their own mouths. All is not theirs,
> it seems;
> One fatal tree there stands, of Knowledge,
> called,
> Forbidden them to taste.[3]

[1] *Anecdota Oxoniensia* (Oxford, 1882).
[2] *Ibid.*, p. 21.   [3] *Paradise Lost*, Bk. IV, ll. 513–15.

Satan's next appearance was when Ithuriel and Ziphon, dispatched by Gabriel, discovered him

> Squat like a toad, close at the ear of Eve. . . . .[1]

That no mere simile was intended here is certain by the next few lines:

> Him thus intent Ithuriel with his spear
> Touched lightly; for no falsehood can endure
> Touch of celestial temper, but returns
> Of force to its own likeness: up he starts,
> Discovered and surprised. . . . .
> So started up in his own shape the Fiend.[2]

That is, the toad was another form in which Satan drew near to his prey, conformable to the rabbinical requirement that he appear in shape displaying his imperfection and abasement, and as Ziphon addressed him:

> and thou resemblest now
> Thy sin and place of doom obscure and foul.[3]

In the form of a toad, Satan almost achieved at least the beginning of the fall of man for which he strove, as the effect of the midnight whispering in the ear of Eve bore fruit two mornings later when she successfully defended her intention of working apart from Adam.

Milton's preparations for the appearance of Satan as a serpent were carefully conceived and elaborately executed. Satan spent much of the time remaining after his escape from the guardian Angel, Gabriel, and after re-entering Paradise, in considering every creature of the earth as to which might best serve his pùrpose. His final selection of the serpent was due to his having had some

[1] *Op. cit.*, Bk. IV, l. 800.
[2] *Op. cit.*, Bk. IV, ll. 810-14, 819.   [3] *Op. cit.*, Bk. IV, ll. 389-40.

experience with most, if not all, other forms of beast, bird, and reptile, in none of which forms had he been able to carry out his design completely and establish contact with the human pair. Milton does not appear to have used the rabbinical fancy that the serpent was the most manlike of the beasts of the earth and hence the most likely tool with which to hold converse with Eve. On the contrary, when, after the Fall, the Curse is laid upon the man, the woman, and the serpent, instead of the suggestions of the rabbis that the serpent now discarded his upright form and assumed that form in which he is now known, Milton expressly states that the serpent was but brute instrument of Satan:

> To judgment he proceeded on the accursed
> Serpent, though brute, unable to transfer
> The guilt on him who made him instrument.[1]

The actual approach of the serpent to Eve was as elaborately staged as had been Satan's selection of instrument, and here again the similarity of Milton's imagery to rabbinic suggestion is striking.

Milton thus describes the Tempter's approach to Eve:

> So spake the enemy of mankind, enclosed
> In serpent, inmate bad, and toward Eve
> Addressed his way, not with indented wave,
> Prone on the ground, as since, but on his rear,
> Circular base of rising folds, that towered
> Fold above fold a surging maze; his head
> Crested aloft, and carbuncle his eyes;
> With burnished neck of verdant gold, erect
> Amidst his circling spires, that on the grass
> Floated redundant. Pleasing was his shape
> And lovely. . . . .[2]

---

[1] *Op. cit.*, Bk. X, ll. 164–66.   [2] *Op. cit.*, Bk. IX, ll. 494 ff.

The rabbinic description of the serpent before the Curse
is as follows:

> Now the serpent was at first the queen of all beasts.
> Her head was like rubies, and her eyes like emerald.
> Her skin shone like a mirror of various hues.
> Her hair was soft like that of a noble virgin;
> and her form resembled the stately camel;
> her breath was like sweet musk and amber;
> and all her words were songs of praise.[1]

The similarity of figure here and in *Paradise Lost* is too
marked to be entirely accidental, and while Milton may
not have used this precise source for his image, he must
have used some later embellishment of it, and his entire
conception of the serpent in the lines quoted is certainly
rabbinical in origin.

A further rabbinical embellishment of the story of the
Fall occurs in the employment of the jealousy motive in
Eve as the impelling force which caused her to induce
Adam to eat also of the forbidden fruit. Saurat has
recently very properly called attention to Milton's knowledge of, and possible indebtedness to, rabbinical writings, and has pointed out a very striking parallel between
Milton's employment of this jealousy motive and that
found in the Zohar. The two passages are as follows:

> But what if God have seen
> And death ensue, then shall I be no more,
> And Adam, wedded to another Eve
> Shall live with her enjoying, I extinct:
> A death to think. Confirmed then I resolve
> Adam shall share with me in bliss or woe:
> So dear I love him that with him all deaths
> I could endure, without him live no life.[2]

[1] Weil, *op. cit.*, translation (London, 1846), p. 9.
[2] *Op. cit.*, Bk. IX, ll. 826–33.

The woman touched the tree. Then she saw the Angel of Death coming toward her, and thought: Perhaps I shall die and the Holy One, Blessed be He, will make another woman and give her to Adam. This must not happen. And she gave the fruit to her husband that he should eat it also (Zohar).[1]

The correspondence here is certainly striking, particularly so in view of the fact that the jealousy motive does not appear in any of the literary treatments of the Garden of Eden story commonly supposed to have been used by Milton. It would, therefore, clearly appear to have been adopted by the poet directly from a rabbinical embroidery of the biblical narrative.

But was it to the Zohar that Milton went for this suggestion? Saurat fails to make a clear or complete case for that particular source, but his suggestion that the jealousy motive was taken from some rabbinical source is well founded, and it is not at all necessary merely to speculate as to Milton's source for the incident. In connection with Salmasius' discussion of the Jewish kings after Maccabaeus in the *Pro Populo Anglicano Defensio* there occurs the following statement:

O te secure mendocem si periisset Josephus restaret tantum Josippus tuus ex quo pharisaeorum quaedem nullus usus apophthegmata depromis.

Milton's reference here is to a work on Jewish history from the Creation to the Maccabean succession, which usually carries the name of Josippon or Yosippon, known throughout the Middle Ages and much later, as his reference suggests, as the pseudo-Josephus. The work is usually mentioned in connection with Joseph ben Gorion and is referred to by Joseph Meade as that of Josephus

[1] Saurat, *op. cit.*, p. 283.

Gorionides. It is not necessary to discuss the perplexities involved in the origins of the work, nor to analyze the immense amount of material contained therein; enough to say that a great many manuscripts exist in Hebrew,[1] and that the first printed edition appeared at Mantua as early as 1476–79.

Moreover, neither Salmasius nor Milton would have had any great difficulty in obtaining access to the work in other than a Semitic form, for as early as 1541 a partial Latin translation appeared at Basle. Another portion was translated into English by Peter Morwyng (London, 1558), and there was a more complete French translation done at Paris in 1609, so that it was comparatively accessible even to the rank and file of the seventeenth-century readers.

The early portions of the work, which deal with the creation of the world and the early history of the Jews, have been admirably arranged and translated into English by Gaster,[2] and it is from this translation that such quotations as are used in this discussion will be made. The particular passage of significance is as follows:

Forthwith Samael, the angel of death, descended and looked at every creature, but he could find none as cunning and malignant as the serpent. The serpent then went to Eve, and began to speak of various things, until he broached the tree. "Is it true," he said, "that God commanded you not to eat of any tree in the garden?" "No, He only forbade us the one tree, which stands in the midst of the garden; we are not allowed to eat of its fruit, nor touch it, for on the day that we touch it we shall die." The serpent then laughed at her, saying, "It is out of jealousy that God has said this for he well knows that if you eat thereof your eyes will be

---

[1] Neubauer, *Jewish Quarterly Review*, XI, 355 ff.

[2] Oriental Translation Fund, 1899, London.

opened, and you will know how to create the world just as he. Indeed, who can believe that for that thou shouldst die? Forsooth, I shall go and pluck some fruit." The serpent accordingly stood on his feet and shook the tree, so that some of the fruit fell upon the ground; and the tree cried, "O wicked one, do not touch me!" When Eve saw the serpent touch the tree and not die, she said to herself, that the words of her husband were false. Therefore, on seeing that the fruit was beautiful, she desired it and ate of it. As soon as she had eaten thereof her teeth were set on edge, and she saw the angel of death with drawn sword standing before her. She then said in her heart, "Woe unto me that I have eaten of this death, for now I will die; and Adam, my husband, who has not eaten of it will live forever, and God will couple him with another woman. It is better that we die together, for God has created us together even unto death." So when her husband came she gave him of the fruit to taste.[1]

The embellishments of the biblical narrative in this account are very significant. The first marked difference from Genesis is when the serpent "began to speak of various things." The Pentateuch mentions no such subtlety. But the *Paradise Lost* parallel is most striking, not only in sequence, but also in idea. Milton has seized on the conception of a casual and subtle apparoach to Eve and expanded it into the gyrations and contortions of the serpent before her, followed by his speeches, which begin with gentle flattery and end by broaching the subject of the tree.

The second parallel is the suggestion put into the mouth of Satan that God imposed a restriction on the Tree of Knowledge out of jealousy toward his creatures (cf. *Paradise Lost*, Bk. IX, 1. 727):

> What can your knowledge hurt him, or this tree
> Impart against his will, if all be his?
> Or is it envy?

[1] Gaster, p. 47.

Yosippon then has the serpent shake the tree, where-upon the tree cries out. There is nothing said in Genesis of anyone's touching the tree, but the motive is, however, at least suggested in Milton, who makes not the serpent, but Eve, stretch forth the hand which calls forth a remonstrance from nature. The parallel passages:

The serpent accordingly stood on his feet and shook the tree, so that some of the fruit fell upon the ground; and the tree cried out "Oh wicked one, do not touch me."

So saying her rash hand in evil hour
Forth reaching to the fruit, she plucked, she eat.
Earth felt the wound, and Nature from her seat
Sighing thro' all her works, gave sign of woe
That all was lost.[1]

The dramatic effect of the incident is undeniably heightened by transferring the action from the fantastical serpent to the human Eve, and Genesis, Yosippon, and Milton all get rid of the serpent as soon as they possibly can, in order to deal with the human element contained in the episode of the Fall. Milton has already advanced the action of the actual connection between the serpent and the tree—which Yosippon has dealt with as the "shaking" of the tree by the serpent—by having the serpent tell Eve that he has already eaten of the fruit.

There is another outstanding parallel between Yosippon and *Paradise Lost*, namely, the soliloquy of Eve before she touches tree or fruit. Here are the passages from each work arranged in parallel columns:

When Eve saw the serpent touch the tree and not die, she said to herself, that the words of her husband were false.

yet first,
Pausing a while, thus to herself she mused . . . .
[follows her soliloquy].[2]

[1] *Op. cit.*, Bk. IX, ll. 780 ff.

[2] *Op. cit.*, Bk. IX, ll. 743 ff.

It will be noticed that both in arrangement and in development the two passages are identical, and the idea contained in the "to herself she mused . . . ." is not contained in the biblical account.

The passage which follows is substantially the same as that given by M. Saurat from the Zohar, and the Miltonic parallel is equally close:

She [Eve] then said in her heart, "Woe unto me that I have eaten of this death, for now I will die; and Adam, my husband, who has not eaten of it will live forever *and God will couple him with another woman*. It is better that we die together, for God has created us together" (Yosippon).

but what if God have seen, And death ensue? Then shall I be no more, And Adam, wedded to another Eve, Shall live with her enjoying, I extinct![1]

Obviously, either account might have supplied Milton with the materials. But the parallels in Yosippon are, as pointed out, more far-reaching than those in the Zohar, comprising not only the jealousy motive, but also the subtlety of the serpent's approach to Eve, the purpose imputed to the Creator in forbidding the fruit, the touching of the tree, with the resultant outcry, the soliloquy of Eve before touching tree or fruit.

Moreover, the most cursory investigation of the attitude of the late Middle Ages, and, indeed, of the seventeenth and eighteenth centuries, toward Yosippon or the pseudo-Josephus will reveal that Milton, in his use of the work as source, is following his invariable procedure in dealing with an authority. His procedure was ever the same. First, he went to the Bible; if the material

[1] *Op. cit.*, Bk. IX, l. 826.

found there was inadequate, or lacking entirely, he then went to the next best authority, or lacking that, to the next, and so on until he had exhausted all possibilities. In all cases when he was dealing with Hebrew text tradition he went from Scripture to Josephus, and it is only reasonable to suppose that in this particular case his next source would be Yosippon, for he himself admitted: *si periisset Josephus restaret tantum Josippus tuus.*

The parallels of the passages are so numerous, the processes of embodiment so typical, and the certainty of Milton's knowledge of the material so beyond question, that the admission of this rabbinical work as a source is almost inevitable.

Thus two of the major conceptions of the poem, the Muse addressed and the entire story of the fall of man, the very heart of the poem, exhibit an indebtedness to Semitic source which is at once definite, peculiar, and of a significant nature.

BIBLIOGRAPHY

BIBLIOGRAPHY
TEXTUAL EDITIONS OF MILTON'S WORKS
PARADISE LOST

MITFORD, J. (editor), *The Works of John Milton in Verse and Prose*, 8 vols., London, 1851.

MASSON, DAVID, *Milton's Poetical Works*, 3 vols., London, 1896.

MOODY, WILLIAM VAUGHN, *The Complete Poetical Works of John Milton*, Boston, 1899.

VERITY, A. W., *Paradise Lost*, Cambridge, 1910.

PARADISE REGAINED AND SAMSON AGONISTES

MITFORD, J., *The Works of John Milton in Verse and Prose*, 8 vols., London, 1851.

MASSON, DAVID, *Milton's Poetical Works*, 3 vols., London, 1896.

MOODY, WILLIAM VAUGHN, *The Complete Poetical Works of John Milton*, Boston, 1899.

MINOR POEMS: ENGLISH, LATIN, GREEK, AND ITALIAN

MILTON, JOHN, *Poems*, 1645, type facsimile, Oxford, 1924.

MILTON, JOHN, *Poems, Etc., upon Several Occasions*, London, 1673.

MITFORD, J., *The Works of John Milton in Verse and Prose*, 8 vols., London, 1851.

MASSON, DAVID, *Milton's Poetical Works*, 3 vols., London, 1896.

MOODY, WILLIAM VAUGHN, *The Complete Poetical Works of John Milton*, Boston, 1899.

PROSE

MILTON, JOHN, *De Doctrina Christiana*, ed. Sumner, London, 1825; *The Christian Doctrine*, translated by Sumner, London, 1825; *The Christian Doctrine*, translated by Sumner, Boston, 1825; the Columbia photostatic copy of the original manuscript.

MITFORD, J., *The Works of John Milton in Verse and Prose*, 8 vols., London, 1851.

BIOGRAPHY

PARSONS, E. S. (editor), "The Earliest Life of Milton," *English Historical Review*, XVII, 95.

AUBREY, J., *Collections for the Life of Milton*, 1681; A. Clark, *Aubrey's Brief Lives* (2 vols., Oxford, 1898), II, 60–70.

WOOD, ANTHONY, "Fasti Oxonienses," in *Athenae Oxonienses* (editor Bliss), London, 1813.

PHILLIPS, EDWARD, *The Life of Milton*, 1694.

TOLAND, JOHN, *The Life of John Milton*, 1698; *Amyntor, or a Defence of Milton's Life*, 1699.

JOHNSON, SAMUEL, "Life of Milton," in *Lives of the Poets*, London, 1779.

KEIGHTLEY, T., *An Account of the Life, Opinions, and Writings of John Milton*, London, 1855.

MASSON, DAVID, *The Life of John Milton*, 7 vols., London, 1858–81.

STERN, ALFRED, *Milton und seine Zeit*, Leipzig, 1877–79.

PATTISON, MARK, *Milton*, London, 1879.

THE SCHOLARSHIP OF THE FIRST HALF OF THE SEVENTEENTH CENTURY

AUBREY, J., *Collections for the Life of Milton*, 1681; A. Clark, *Aubrey's Brief Lives* (2 vols., Oxford, 1898), II, 60–70.

BAILLET, A., *Jugemens des Savans*, 8 vols., Paris, 1725.

BASIRE, ISAAC, *Correspondence in the Reigns of Charles I and Charles II, and Memoir* (editor, W. N. Darnell), 1831.

BEARD, C., *The Reformation of the Sixteenth Century in Its Relation to Modern Thought and Knowledge*, Hibbert Lectures, 1883.

BEGLEY, WALTER, *Nova Solyma*, 1648 (1902).

BIRCH, U., *Anna van Schurman*, 1909.

BOWES, R., *Catalog of Books Printed at, or Relating to, Cambridge*, 1894.

BRUGGEMANN, L. W., *View of the English Editions, Translations and Illustrations of the Ancient Greek and Latin Authors*, Stettin, 1797.

BURNET, GILBERT, *Life of Sir Matthew Hale*, 1682.

CALAMY, EDMUND, *Nonconformist's Memorial* (editor, Samuel Palmer), 2 vols., 1802–3.

BIBLIOGRAPHY 143

CATTERMOLE, R., *Literature of the Church of England*, 2 vols., 1844.

CHILD, GILBERT W., *Church and State under the Tudors*, 1890.

CHRISTIE, R. C., *The Old Church and School Libraries of Lancashire*, Chetham Society Publications, n.s., Vol. VII, 1885.

COX, ROBERT, *The Literature of the Sabbath Question*, 2 vols., 1865.

DEXTER, H. M., AND MORTON, *The England and Holland of the Pilgrims*, 1906.

DIBDIN, T. F., *An Introduction to the Knowledge of Rare and Valuable Editions of the Greek and Latin Classics*, 2 vols., 1827.

DIRCKS, HENRY, *A Biographical Memoir of Samuel Hartlib, with Bibliographical Notices*, 1865.

FELL, JOHN, *Life of Sir Matthew Hale and Life of Henry Hammond*, Oxford, 1856.

GROWOLL, A., AND EAMES, W., *Three Centuries of English Book Trade Bibliography*, New York, 1903.

HACKET, JOHN, *Scrinia Reserata*, 2 vols., 1693.

HEYWOOD, J., *Cambridge University Transactions during the Puritan Controversies of the Sixteenth and Seventeenth Centuries*, 2 vols., 1854.

LAURIE, S. S., *Studies in the History of Educational Opinions*, 1905.

MADAN, FALCONER, *The Early Oxford Press*, Oxford, 1895.

MAYOR, J. E. B., *Autobiography of Matthew Robinson*, 1856.

MIDDLETON, ERASMUS, *Biographia Evangelica*, 4 vols., 1779.

MITCHELL, A. F., *The Westminster Assembly*, Baird Lectures, 1883.

MOORE, NORMAN, *History of the Study of Medicine in the British Isles*, 1908.

MORHOF, D. G., *Polyhistor Literarius*, Lubecae, 1714.

MULLINGER, J. BASS, *Cambridge Characteristics in the Seventeenth Century*, 1867; *The University of Cambridge*, 1884.

PARKINSON, REV. CANON R., *Life of Adam Martindale*, Chetham Society Publications, 1845.

PARR, RICHARD, *Life of James Usher*, 1686.

PATTISON, MARK, *Isaac Casaubon*, 2d ed., 1892.

QUICK, R. H., *Essays on Educational Reformers*, 1868.

SANDYS, J. E., *A History of Classical Scholarship*, Vol. II, 1908.

SCHICKLER, LE BARON F. DE, *Les églises du refuge en Angleterre*, 3 vols., Paris, 1892.

SHAW, W. A., *History of the English Church during the Civil War and under the Commonwealth*, 2 vols., 1900.

SMITH, PHILIP A., *History of Education for the English Bar*, 1860.

TODD, H. J., *Brian Walton*, 2 vols., 1821.

UNDERHILL, J. G., *Spanish Literature in the England of the Tudors*, 1899.

WALKER, JOHN, *The Sufferings of the Clergy*, 1714.

WALTON, JOSEPH, *Early History of Legal Studies in England*, 1900.

WASE, CHRISTOPHER, *Considerations concerning Free Schools, as Settled in England*, 1678.

WORTHINGTON, DR. JOHN, *Diary and Correspondence*, Chetham Society Publications, Vols. XIII and XXXVI.

YOUNG, SIR GEORGE, *History of Greek Literature in England from the Earliest Times to the End of the Reign of James I*, 1862.

CONTEMPORARY HEBREW GRAMMARS

REUCHLIN, JOHANN, *Rudimenta Linguae Hebraicae*, Pforzheim, 1506.

CAPITO, W. F., *Institutiuncula in Hebr. Linguam*, Basel, 1516.

MÜNSTER, SEBASTIAN, *Epitome Hebr. Grammaticae*, Basel, 1520.

PAGNINUS, SANCTUS, *Institutiones Hebraicae*, Lyons, 1520.

TREMELLIUS, EMANUEL, *Rudimenta Linguae Hebr.*, Wittenberg, 1541.

MARTINIUS, PETRUS, *Gramm. Hebr.*, Paris, 1568.

SCHINDLERUS, VALENTIUS, *Instit. Hebr.*, Wittenberg, 1575.

BELLARMINUS, ROBERTUS, *Instit. Linguae Hebr.*, Rome, 1578.

JUNIUS, FRANCISCUS, *Gr. Hebr. Linguae*, Frankfort, 1580.

UDAL, JOHN, *The Key of the Holy Scriptures* (translations from Martinius), Leyden, 1593.

BUXTORF, JOHANN (I), *Praecepta Gramm. Hebr.*, Basel, 1605 (17 editions by 1675).

AMAMA, SIXTUS. *Gramm. Hebr.*, Amsterdam, 1625.

TROSTIUS, MARTINUS. *Gramm. Hebr. Universalis*, Copenhagen, 1627.

CONTEMPORARY LEXICONS

REUCHLIN, JOHANNES, *Rudimenta Linguae Hebr. una cum Lexico*, Pforzheim, 1506.

MÜNSTER, SEBASTIAN, *Dictionarum Hebr.*, Basel, 1529.

PAGNINUS, SANCTUS, *Thesaurus Linguae Sanctae*, Leyden, 1529; *Epitome*, Antwerp, 1570.

BUXTORF, JOHANN (I), *Lexicon Hebr.-Chald.*, Basel, 1607 (11 editions by 1675).

SCHINDLERUS, VALENTINUS, *Lexicon Pentaglotton, Hebr., Chald., Syr., Talmudic-Rabbin., et Arab.*, Frankfort, 1612.

AMAMA, SIXTUS, *Hebrew Lexicon* (Dutch), Franeker, 1628.

ALABASTER, WILLIAM, *Spiraculum Tubarum*, London, 1635.

LEIGH, EDWARD, *Critica Sacra*, London, 1639.

CASTELL, EDWARD, *Lexicon Heptaglotton*, London, 1669 (for the Walton Polyglot).

LEXICONS FOR THE TALMUD AND RABBINICAL LITERATURE

MÜNSTER, SEBASTIAN, *Dictionarium Chaldaicum*, Basel, 1527.

BUXTORF, JOHANN (I), *Lexicon Chaldaicum, Talmudicum* (edited by Johann II), Basel, 1639.

CONTEMPORARY WORKS OF GENERAL LEARNING

BREREWOOD, EDWARD, *Enquiries Touching the Diversity of Languages and Religion through the Chief Parts of the World*, 1614.

BRINSLEY, JOHN, *Ludus Literarius of the Grammar Schoole*, 1612.

DURY, JOHN, *Reformed School*, 1650.

HALES, JOHN, *Golden Remains*, 1659.

HEYLYN, PETER, *Cosmographie in Four Bookes*, 1652.

HOOLE, CHARLES, *New Discovery of the Old Art of Teaching School*, 1660.

LONDON, WILLIAM, *A Catalogue of the Most Vendible Books in England*, 1658.

MINSHEU, JOHN, *The Guide into Tongues*, 1617.

HOLINSHED, RALPH, *Historie of England*, London, 1808.

RALEIGH, SIR WALTER, *History of the World*, 1614.

SANDYS, EDWIN, *Europe Speculum*, Paris, 1599.

PURCHAS, SAMUEL. *His Pilgrimage*, London, 1617.

MORE, SIR HENRY, *Philosophical Writings*, 4th ed., 1712.

HAKEWELL, GEORGE, *An Apologie of Declaration of the Power and Providence of God*, London, 1627, 1635.

CHILLINGWORTH, WILLIAM, *The Religion of Protestants*, 1637.

GALE, THEOPHILUS, *Court of the Gentiles*, 1669–77.

GLANVIL, JOSEPH, *Sadducismus Triumphatus*, 1681.

POOLE, MATHEW, *Synopsis Criticorum Bibliorum*, 5 vols., 1660–1676.

BAXTER, RICHARD, *Reliquiae Baxterianae*.

JONES, WHARTON T., *William Bedell*, Camden Society Publications, 1872.

BURTON, ROBERT, *Anatomy of Melancholy*, 1621.

CASAUBON, MERIC, *Commentary on the Hebrew and [Anglo-] Saxon Language*, 1650.

CUDWORTH, RALPH, *Intellectual System*, 1678.

CULVERWEL, NATHANIEL, *On the Nature of Light*, 1652.

GATAKER, THOMAS, *Annotations on the Bible*, 1659.

SELDEN, JOHN, *Opera*, 6 vols., 1726.

GRAFTON, RICHARD, *Chronicle or History of England*, 1809 (1611).

LILLY, WILLIAM, *Monarchy or No Monarchy*. Reprinted in F. Masseres, *Select Tracts*, Part 1, 1815.

BIBLES

Breeches Bible, Geneva, 1560.

Cf. *Notes and Queries*, 11, III, 109.

BUXTORF, JOHANN (I), *Biblia Sacra, Hebraica, et Chaldaica*, Basel, 1620.

TREMELLIUS, IMMANUEL, AND JUNIUS, FRANCISCO, *Biblia Sacra*, Genevae, 1617.

WRIGHT, WILLIAM ALDIS, *The Authorized Version of the English Bible*, 1611, 5 vols., Cambridge, 1909.

WALTON, BRIAN, AND OTHERS, *Biblia Sacra Polyglotta*, 6 vols., 1657.

TISCHENDORF, CONSTANTINUS DE, *Biblia Sacra Latina*, Lipsiae, 1873.

BROOKE, ALAN E., AND MCLEAN, NORMAN, *The Old Testament in Greek*, Cambridge, 1917.

WRIGHT, WILLIAM ALDIS, *The Hexaplar Psalter*, Cambridge, 1911.

KITTEL, RUD., *Biblia Hebraica*, Stutgart, 1912.

WESTCOTT, B. F., AND HORT, F. J., *The New Testament in the Original Greek*, 1881.

DIODATI, GIOVANNI, *La Sacra Biblia*, edition of London, 1844.

THOMAS YOUNG

HOLLINGSWORTH, A. G. H., *The History of Stowmarket*, London, 1844, pp. 187–195.
MASSON, DAVID, *Life of Milton*, Vol. I, 1881.

ST. PAUL'S SCHOOL AND THE GRAMMAR SCHOOLS

BRINSLEY, JOHN, *Ludus Literarius*, 1612.
——, *A Consolation for Our Grammar Schooles.*
CARLISLE, N., *A Concise Description of the Endowed Grammar Schools in England and Wales*, 2 vols., 1818.
CHURTON, RALPH, *Life of Alex. Nowell, Dean of St. Paul's*, 1809.
HEARNE, T., *Reliquianae* (editor, Bliss), 2 vols., 1857.
LEACH, A. F., *The Schools of Medieval England*, London, 1915.
——, *Educational Charters and Documents*, Cambridge, 1911.
——, *English Schools at the Reformation*, 1894.
——, "Free Grammar Schools," *National Observer*, September–October, 1896.
——, "The Ancient Schools in the City of London," in Sir Walter Besant's *London, the City*, London, 1910.
——, "St. Paul's School," London, *The Times*, April 2 and 12, 1904.
——, "St. Paul's School," *Journal of Education*, July, 1909.
——, "Milton as Schoolboy and Schoolmaster," *Proceedings British Academy*, III, 1909.
——, "St. Paul's School before Colet," *Archaeologia*, LXII (1910–11), 191; cf. also *The Times*, July 7, 14, August 3, 1909.
LUPTON, J. H., *Life of Dean Colet*, 1909.
MCDONNELL, M. F. J., *History of St. Paul's School*, 1909.
MULCASTER, RICHARD, *Positions*, 1581 (editor, Quick), 1888.
POLLARD, A. F., *England under the Protector Somerset*, 1900.
STAUNTON, HOWARD, *The Great Schools of England.*
WATSON, FOSTER, *The English Grammar Schools to 1660*, 1908.

THE PSALMS

WRIGHT, W. A., *The Hexaplar Psalter*, Cambridge, 1911.
TISCHENDORF, C. DE, *Biblia Sacra Latina*, Lipsiae, 1873.
WALTON, BRIAN, *Biblia Sacra Polyglotta*, 6 vols., 1657.

KITTEL, RUD., *Biblia Hebraica*, Stuttgart, 1912.

TREMELLIUS, EMANUEL, AND FRANCISCO, JUNIUS, *Biblia Sacra*, Genevae, 1617.

CHEYNE, T. K., *The Book of Psalms*, London, 1904.

Douay Version of the Old Testament, translated from the Latin Vulgate by the Roman Catholic College of Douay, 1609, Baltimore, 1889.

DIODATI, GIOVANNI, *La Sacra Biblia*, London, 1844.

AINSWORTH, HENRY, *Psalms in Metre* (edition of 1642), 1612.

BARTON, WILLIAM, *The Booke of Psalmes in Metre*, edition of 1682.

BRATHWAITE, RICHARD, *The Psalms of David*, London, 1638.

BUCHANAN, GEORGE, *Psalmorum Davidis paraphrasis poetica*, 1566 (1715).

——, "Buchanan's Psalms," in *George Buchanan: A Memorial*, by Allan Menzies, St. Andrews, 1907, p. 136.

ROUS, FRANCIS, *Psalms*, edition of 1673.

SANDYS, GEORGE, *Paraphrase upon the Psalmes*, edition of 1636.

STERNHOLD AND HOPKINS, *The Whole Book of Psalmes*, edition of 1619.

WITHER, GEORGE, *The Psalms of David*, edition of 1632, Spenser Society.

HEBREW WORKS

BUXTORF, JOHANN, ed., Maimonides, (Moses ben Maimon), *Doctor Perplexorum*, Basel, 1629.

GASTER, M., *The Chronicle of Jerahmeel*, Oriental Translation Fund, 1899.

"The Book of the Bee," *Anecdota Oxoniensia*, Oxford, 1882.

WÜNSCHE, AUGUST, *Der Midrasch Bereschit Rabba*, Leipsig, 1881.

JOSEPHUS, *The Antiquities of the Jews*, 4 vols., ed., Whiston, London, 1825.

SCHECHTER, S., *Mildrasch Haggadol*, Cambridge, 1902.

WEIL, G., *Biblische legenden der Muselmänner*, 1845.

MIGNE, *Enc. Theol.*

Masorah of the Buxtorf *Biblia Sacra*.

RODKINSON, M. L., *The Babylonian Talmud*, New York, 1902.

BARTOLOCCIUS, JULIUS, *Vitae celebrium Rabbinorum*, 1702.

——, *Bibliotheca magna Rabbinorum*, Rome, 1675–94.

GENERAL INTRODUCTIONS TO THE PERIOD

Reign of Charles I, Commonwealth and Protectorate, Calendar of State Papers, Domestic Series.

LILLY, WILLIAM, *Monarchy or No Monarchy in England.* Reprinted in F. Masseres, *Select Tracts,* Part 1, 1815.

PATER, WALTER, *The Renaissance,* 1873.

SMITH, LOGAN PEARSALL, *The Life and Letters of Sir Henry Wotton,* Oxford, 1907.

TAYLOR, H. O., *Thought and Expression in the Sixteenth Century,* 2 vols., New York, 1920.

——, *The Medieval Mind,* 2 vols., New York, 1919.

THURLOE, J., *Collection of State Papers,* 7 vols., 1742.

TULLOCK, JOHN, *Rational Theology and Christian Philosophy in England in the Seventeenth Century,* 2 vols., 1872.

WHARTON, T. J., *William Bedell,* Camden Society Publications, 1872.

RECENT BOOKS

BAILEY, M. L., *Milton and Jakob Boehme,* New York, 1914.

HAVENS, D. H., *The Influence of Milton on English Poetry,* Harvard University Press, 1922.

LILJEGREN, S. B., *Studies in Milton,* Lund, 1918.

MUTSCHMANN, H., *Der andere Milton,* Bonn, 1920.

——, *Milton und das Licht,* Halle, 1920.

SAURAT, DENIS, *Milton: Man and Thinker,* New York, 1925.

SMART, J. S., *The Sonnets of Milton,* Glasgow, 1921.

THOMPSON, E. N., S., *John Milton* (topical bibliography), New Haven, 1916.

RECENT PERIODICAL ARTICLES

BALDWIN, E. C., "Milton and the Psalms," *Modern Philology,* XVII, 457.

——, "Milton and Ezekiel," *Modern Language Notes,* XXXIII (April, 1918), 211.

——, "Milton and Plato's *Timaeus,*" *Publications Modern Language Association,* XXXV, 210.

——, "The Authorized Version's Influence upon Milton's Diction," *Modern Language Notes,* XXXVI, 376.

BREDVOLD, L. I., "Milton and Bodin's *Heptaplomeres,*" *Studies in Philology,* XXI, 399.

DODGE, R. E. NEIL, "Theology in *Paradise Lost*," *University of Wisconsin Studies in Language and Literature*, 1918, No. 2, p. 9.

ERSKINE, JOHN, "The Theme of Death in Paradise Lost," *Publications Modern Language Association*, XXXII (December, 1917), 573.

FLETCHER, H. F., "Milton and Yosippon," *Studies in Philology*, XXI, 496.

GILBERT, A. H., "Milton on the Position of Women," *Modern Language Review*, XV, 7 and XV, 240.

——, "The Problem of Evil in *Paradise Lost*," *Journal of English and German Philology*, XXII, 175.

——, "Milton's Textbook of Astronomy," *Publications Modern Language Association*, XXXVIII, 290.

——, "The Cambridge Manuscript and Milton's Plans for an Epic," *Studies in Philology*, XVI, 172.

——, "Milton and Galileo," *Studies in Philology*, XIX, 152.

HANFORD, J. H., "The Date of Milton's *De doctrina Christiana*," *Studies in Philology*, XVII, 309.

——, "The Arrangement and Dates of Milton's Sonnets," *Modern Philology*, XVIII, 475.

——, "The Chronology of Milton's Private Studies," *Publications Modern Language Association*, XXXVI, 251.

——, "The Temptation Motive in Milton," *Studies in Philology*, XV, 176.

——, "Milton and the Return to Humanism," *Studies in Philology*, XVI, 126.

HÜBENER, G., "Milton's Satan," *Englische Studien*, LV, 136.

LILJEGREN, S. B., "La pensée de Milton et Giordano Bruno," *Revue de Littérature Comparative*, III, 516.

LOWENHAUPT, W. H., "The Writings of Milton's *Eikonoklastes*," *Studies in Philology*, XX, 29.

MUTSCHMANN, H., "Toland und Milton," *Beiblatt zur Anglia*, XXXII, 87.

RAND, E. K., "Milton in Rustication," *Studies in Philology*, XIX, 315.

THOMPSON, E. N. S., "A Forerunner of Milton," *Modern Language Notes*, XXXII (December, 1917), 479.

——, "Milton's *Of Education*," *Studies in Philology*, XV, 159.

——, "Mysticism in Seventeenth-Century English Literature," *Studies in Philology*, XVIII, 170.

INDEX

INDEX

Mirandola, 6
More, Sir Thomas, 32
Mulcaster, Richard, 33, 35, 38, 40
Muse of Milton's Song, 115 ff.

Newport Grammar School (Essex), 34
Nine Psalms Done into Meter, 16, 63, 97 ff.

Of Education, 16, 26, 35, 36, 78, 80

Pagnine's Hebrew Lexicon, 39
Pattison, Mark, 10
Persian, 40, 89
Persian Astrology, 6
Phillips, Edward, 16, 41, 78, 80
Playfere, Thomas, 9
Pococke, Edward, 48, 89
Pro populo Anglicano defensio, 63, 86, 133
Psalm 114, 53, 99

Rabbinical Hebrew, 20, 77, 79
Rashi, 75
Reason of Church Government, 23, 25
Renaissance, 6
Reuchlin, Johann, 6
Rous, Francis, 108

St. Anthony's Free School, 32
St. Paul's School, 24, 26, 32 ff.
Salmasius, 87, 133
Samael (סמאל), 127, 134
Samaritan, 40, 48, 60, 89
Satan, 111, 126, 127 ff.
Saurat, Denis, 121, 132
Scaligers, The, 8
Schindler's Hebrew Lexicon, 40

Selden, John, 13, 93
Septuagint, 20, 72, 73, 75, 84, 89
Serpent, 126 ff.
Shekinah (שכינה), 122 ff.
Spalding, Robert, 47, 49 n.
Sternhold and Hopkins Psalter, 102 ff., 108
Syriac, 16, 35, 40, 48 n., 56, 59, 60, 80–81

Talmud, 60, 86 f., 123
Targums, 16, 46, 59, 60, 74, 75, 78, 79, 91, 101, 106, 123
Tetrachordon, 46 n., 80, 101 n.
Tovey, Nathaniel, 51, 54
Tremellius, Emanuel, 44–45, 60 n., 69, 72, 80, 83, 100
Trost, Martin, Hebrew Grammar, 40

Udall, John, 49 n.
Urania, 116 f.
Usher, James, 49, 88

Vatablus, Francis, 46 and n., 91–92
Vondel's *Lucifer*, 112
Vulgate, 20, 79, 83–84, 89, 100

Wakefield, Thomas, 43, 47
Walton, Brian, 46, 48 and n., 80 n., 84, 88 ff., 91, 101
Westminster School, 32, 34, 39
Whelocke, Abraham, 48 n., 90
Whitgift, Archbishop, 32, 47

York School, 34
Young, Patrick, 90
Young, Thomas, 14, 24, 27 ff., 36, 41, 42, 52–53, 75

Ziphon, 130